More praise for *Plenty in Life is Free*

Kathy Sdao does a GREAT job of dispelling the myth of NILIF! After all, aren't dogs supposed to be our "best friends"?

Patricia McConnell, PhD, CAAB, author of *Love Has No Age Limit*

I have never read a book about animal training quite like this one! Kathy's approach is part memoir, part philosophy, and full of practical training advice. She makes a hard-hitting and compelling argument for the use of compassion in training and the reasons why so many well-practiced training beliefs should be reconsidered and changed. Her approach is brutally honest, always fair, very practical, at times uncomfortably thought-provoking, and full of wisdom that all dog owners and trainers, professional or amateur, should read. The things I will take away from this quick and enjoyable read are too plentiful to list here without practically recounting the entire book.

Ken Ramirez, Executive Vice President of Animal Care & Training Shedd Aquarium, Chicago, author of *Animal Training: Successful Animal Management through Positive Reinforcement*

In her beautifully written book, *Plenty in Life is Free,* Kathy Sdao systematically debunks one of the most dangerous myths in the dog world today—that nothing should be given a dog unless he "earns" it in some way. She presents the scientific principles behind her beliefs though her words are imbued with a sense of grace and caring. It wasn't just a pleasure to read, it was a privilege.

Jennifer Arnold, Founder of Canine Assistants, *New York Times* bestselling author of *Through a Dog's Eyes* and *In a Dog's Heart*

Sdao's book is a unique combination of soul-searching, self evaluation, humor, and empathy. Kathy openly guides the reader through her thought process to unravel the NILIF modality that has been a popular treatment protocol in dog training. She invites us to consider the ethics and efficacy of these dogmatic practices and builds a strong case that some things in life are free, and SHOULD be free, as she explores our bonds with not only dogs, but other living beings. Kathy then empowers us with alternatives that get results while deepening the joy of the human/canine partnership by incorporating "See, Mark, Reward" in our daily lives. I would suggest that this book is a spiritual awakening for all dog lovers.

Dana C. Crevling, CPDT, CNWI, owner of Dogs of Course

Dedication

To Dr. Patricia D. Ebert
(1950 – 1985)

PLENTY IN LIFE IS FREE

Reflections on Dogs, Training and Finding Grace

Kathy Sdao, ACAAB

Wenatchee, WA

ABERDEENSHIRE LIBRARIES

1971005

Plenty in Life is Free
Reflections on Dogs, Training and Finding Grace
Kathy Sdao, ACAAB

Dogwise Publishing
A Division of Direct Book Service, Inc.
403 South Mission Street, Wenatchee, Washington 98801
509-663-9115, 1-800-776-2665
www.dogwisepublishing.com / info@dogwisepublishing.com

© 2012 Kathy Sdao, ACAAB

Graphic design: Lindsay Peternell
Photos courtesy of Jon Smith, www.jonsmithphotos.com

All rights reserved. No part of this book may be reproduced or transmitted in any form or by any means, electronic, digital or mechanical, including photo-copying, recording or by any information storage or retrieval system without permission in writing from the publisher.

Limits of Liability and Disclaimer of Warranty:
The authors and publisher shall not be liable in the event of incidental or con-sequential damages in connection with, or arising out of, the furnishing, per-formance, or use of the instructions and suggestions contained in this book.

ISBN 978-1617810-64-0

Library of Congress Cataloging-in-Publication Data
Sdao, Kathy.
  Plenty in life is free : reflections on dogs, training and finding grace / by Kathy Sdao.
    p. cm.
  Includes bibliographical references.
  ISBN 978-1-61781-064-0
  1. Dogs--Training. 2. Dogs--Behavior. 3. Dogs--Psychology. 4. Sdao, Kathy. 5. Dog trainers--United States--Biography. 6. Human-animal rela-tionships--United States. 7. Grace (Theology) 8. Spiritual life. I. Title.
  SF431.S397 2012
  636.7'0887--dc23

                               2012000431

Printed in the U.S.A.

"Cows were sacred;
dogs were not."

Cutting for Stone by Abraham Verghese (2009)

TABLE OF CONTENTS

ACKNOWLEDGMENTS

Ah karma. It's cosmic justice that I should rack my brain to try to include everyone who's facilitated the birth of this book. That's because I've been guilty of checking the "Acknowledgments" section of colleagues' books to see if they noted my contribution, tiny though it was. Now I'm faced with the sure knowledge that I will neglect to include at least a few significant supporters, both because my mind is sometimes a sieve and because this book's gestation period exceeded that of an elephant calf.

Taped on the wall next to my writing desk is a printed version of the exuberantly encouraging email sent to me by Dana Crevling—dear friend, owner of *Dogs of Course,* and sponsor of many of my seminars—when I, at about mile twenty-three of my writing marathon, was flagging. In several regards, Dana has been my early adopter; she saw talent in me before even I did. From the beginning, from afar, both Dana and Carolyn Barney have ceaselessly cheered me on in this writing adventure.

Treasured friend and colleague Dorothy Turley eased me through several stuck points, and, as she's done over many years and at multiple gigs, she contributed insight and helped me see more clearly.

In my desk drawer, together with other electronic equipment my iPhone has rendered defunct, lies the small Sony cassette-recorder my friend Shauna Shipley gave me years ago. She knew it would encourage me to preserve, and eventually write up, some of my animal-training anecdotes. Even more generously, Shauna has frequently volunteered her time and her expertise as an instructional designer to help me create effective and fun seminars. These teaching opportunities paved the way for this book.

My sister Cheryl Nowak, newspaper owner and professional editor, generously sacrificed a chunk of her vacation to review the manuscript. Her consummate skill and care made this a better book and saved me some embarrassment. The remaining errors are, of course, all mine.

An abundance of other folks provided sustenance or inspiration along the way. I'm grateful for these kind souls. They include Louisa Beal, Eva Bertilsson, Karen Bream, Linda Brodzik, Virginia Broitman, Kelli Brooke, Sue Coller, John Fuchs, Jim Harbaugh, Ann Howie, Nancy Kedward, Sherrie Kilborn, Alexandra Kurland, Steve Lantry, Karri Lee, Sherri Lippman, Terri Mallett, Harriet Mooney, Suzi Moore, Joan Orr, Susan Pierce, Michele Pouliot, Ken Ramirez, Lori Salo, Shannon & Jon Smith, Liane Sperlich, Lori Stevens, Anita Valigura and Emelie Johnson Vegh.

I also offer sincere thanks to everyone who has attended one of my training seminars or workshops over the past decade. Your enthusiastic and gracious feedback reinforced the idea that I might have something useful to say.

I cannot imagine a better team to collaborate with than the dedicated folks at Dogwise. It was almost exactly two years ago when I met Jon Luke at a conference. He suggested that I might have a book in me. Through subsequent conversations, Jon enabled me to believe this too. Later, Larry Woodward contributed his vast expertise as both an editor and a publisher. I liken the incredible patience Larry and Jon demonstrated with me, a fledgling writer with more fears than fluency, to that of a skilled trainer working with a skittish dog. They never pressured me, but instead offered encouragement and extra time so I could move along at my own pace.

By all this and more, I'm blessed beyond reason.

FOREWORD

Over breakfast at the ClickerExpo, Kathy shared with me the struggle she was having organizing the first draft of her book. She needn't have worried. Kathy has written a gem of a book. Engaging, thought-provoking—these are such cliché terms, I hesitate to use them, but they fit so perfectly. In *Plenty in Life is Free,* Kathy asks us to question what we've been taught about animal training. She challenges us to look beyond the standard answers and the superficial layers of training to examine our core beliefs about training, about animals, and ultimately about ourselves. If this sounds like heavy going, don't worry. From the first sentence on, Kathy charms us with her easy writing style, her stories, and the strong convictions she holds about animals. This book is a breath of fresh air. She doesn't bully us into thinking we have to dominate our animal friends. She doesn't over-complicate her narrative with the lingo of the professional trainer. Instead she makes a clear case for replacing the "Nothing in Life is Free" training mindset with an approach that creates something else Kathy and I have had conversations about—an emotionally intact animal.

I first met Kathy in 1998. She was presenting at the APDT (Association of Pet Dog Trainers) conference. During her presentation, she shared the story of E.T., the walrus she worked with at Point

Defiance Zoo & Aquarium in Tacoma WA. I've sat through count-less presentations, but only a few stick. Kathy's had super-glue at-tached to it. I encountered more of her super-glue when I watched her "Moment of Science" presentations at the ClickerExpo. Kathy is a dynamic presenter and a wonderful story-teller. That helps to make a presentation interesting, but that's not enough to create super-glue. Kathy's real skill is the ability to look at complex subjects and to dis-till out of them the essential elements we need to understand them. Kathy brings these same super-glue skills to her new book.

I feel very privileged that I've been able to know Kathy not just as a presenter, but also as a friend. We've both been on the ClickerExpo faculty since its inception. At these gatherings, we get to indulge in a mutual passion—talking about training and animals. I work with horses. Kathy works with dogs. But we're both clicker trainers. What is the same? What is different? Certainly there are differences in techniques, but that's not the layer of training that matters. Reading *Plenty in Life is Free,* I see so very clearly that at the core we both want the same thing. When we look at our animal friends, we want to see a sparkle in their eyes, we want to know that there's still "someone at home." I remember conversations in which Kathy talked about wanting an emotionally intact dog. Dogs make her smile. Happy, wiggly, enthusiastic dogs delight her. That doesn't mean dogs with no manners who lack the training to fit into a house full of humans. But it does mean that the personality of the dog is treasured, and the physical and emotional needs of the dog are fully met.

In the horse world, we encounter a similar insistence on being the leader that is also preached in dog training. In *Plenty in Life is Free,* Kathy questions what this means and the effect it has on the rela-tionships between people and their animal companions. She offers a clear, easy-to-follow alternative to this dominant and dominating training system. I know my horses would feel right at home in a household run by Kathy. They might not fit on her couch, but I know they would find space in her heart.

Alexandra Kurland
Author of *Clicker Training for Your Horse; The Click That Teaches: A Step-By Step Guide in Pictures; The Click That Teaches: Riding with the Clicker;* and *The Click That Teaches: DVD Lesson Series.*

INTRODUCTION

You've surely heard the purported Chinese curse, "May you live in interesting times." I've been supremely blessed to have lived in interesting jobs for thirty years. As a contractor for the United States Department of Defense, I trained bottlenosed dolphins to locate and neutralize deep-moored mines in the open ocean. As a research assistant at the University of Hawaii's Kewalo Basin Marine Mammal Laboratory, I helped teach sign-language to other dolphins. As a zookeeper in my current hometown of Tacoma, Washington, I cared for rarely-seen harbor porpoises, gentle beluga whales and a magnificent two-ton walrus named E.T. I crewed on a large motorsailer during a week-long dolphin collecting trip in the waters off the Big Island of Hawaii. I even traveled to Paris, just after the 9/11 terrorist attacks, for a dog-sitting gig. My first job, however, was as a Hooker. Sort of. More on this in the next chapter.

I'm now nearly 50 years old. If I squint, I can see the half-century milestone anchored around the next bend, forever casting me out of anyone's notion of "young adult." Along with plenty of character lines around my eyes and mental voids into which acquaintances' names and common English words slip with alarming frequency, I've developed a profusion of gray hair. For now, I'm keeping the salt in my pepper-colored locks, mostly because I've earned it (and, less dramatically, because my last dye job was ghastly).

Shades of grays

I've come to realize that I'm more willing to accommodate other gray areas, too. Instead of clinging to certainty about, well, everything, I've started pitching a few philosophical tents on slippery slopes. I've also found some secure ledges. For example, I, a proud liberal in almost every way, now empathize with at least one concern of National Rifle Association (NRA) members. One day, years ago, reflecting on how foolish it was that my city had outlawed off-leash dog parks, I realized that NRA folks feel about guns the way I feel about dogs: for my own peace of mind I need them in my life, despite the fact that some are dangerous and may, especially in the hands of uneducated owners, occasionally injure innocent people. (I haven't fallen completely over the NRA cliff; bans on assault rifles are irrefutable, in my opinion.) My black-or-white viewpoint that "guns are bad" has developed into a more slate-toned stance. And yes, perching on this slippery slope, working to maintain balance, embracing the murky middle-ground, is a whole lot less comfortable than sitting securely on the top of the hill.

Now, in many other ways, I hang on to fewer absolutes, though this change has been fitful and fraught. I agree with writer Anne Lamott's admission: "Everything I let go of has claw marks on it." Yet, over time, the bravado and arrogance of knowing damn near everything when I was 25 years old has morphed into a willingness to admit just how much I'm unsure of. Twice as old, half as certain. But, with five decades of living in the rear-view mirror, perhaps a bit wiser as well.

Growing older has changed the way I train dogs and view my relationship with them. While I always have been associated with a training philosophy that avoids coercion and physical force (force is not much of an option when your animal weighs 10 times more than you and swims 1,000 times better than you), there is one particular tenet of positive-training philosophy that I've wrestled with: Nothing in Life Is Free (NILIF). This is the dictum that dogs should be required to earn all privileges and rewards by first performing a behavior (e.g., "Sit") requested by a human. It turns out that my concerns with NILIF have at least as much to do with my own spirituality and personal view of relationships as with the pros and cons of NILIF as a training regimen.

I'm entirely aware how odd it is to discuss spirituality in a book about dog training. And though I suspect there are other animal trainers and veterinary professionals concerned with the issues I'll discuss, this is not a book which focuses on the intersection of faith and training. Instead, it offers a critique of NILIF and suggests alternative frameworks for dog training. First, let me explain why this is so important to me.

CHAPTER 1
Doubt of Control

All animal training is, to some extent, inherently manipulative. We trainers strive to control events and environmental stimuli to create behavioral changes in our animals. The best trainers do this skillfully, minimizing any pressure or distress the animal experiences during the learning process. Less-great trainers do this using force—both physical and psychological—to compel their animals to act correctly. Recently, I've come to admit that I've always been a master manipulator, though I rejected this assessment when I first heard it as a teenager.

My first job, as a 16-year-old in my childhood home of Niagara Falls, New York, was working as a painter at the local Hooker Chemical plant. This name seems comical—I wore an orange T-shirt emblazoned with "Hooker" in big black block letters—unless you know about Love Canal, the environmental disaster named for the suburban neighborhood where Hooker Chemical buried more than 20,000 tons of toxic waste.

I was one of a dozen teens hired to work summers painting the exteriors of buildings and chemical tanks. Each kid was the son or daughter of a Hooker Chemical employee; the summer job was a perk allotted to some of the senior workers there. I was the exception; my dad didn't work at the plant, but he did have clout—he was the Niagara Falls city manager.

Looking back, it's shocking to realize how truly hazardous this job was. We each wore a hard hat and steel-toed boots and on a belt around our waists hung an in-case-of-chemical-leak gas mask. I had an eerily close brush with death at that facility, as I barely missed being sprayed with corrosive chemicals that burst from a hose that ruptured while workers loaded a tank car.

Each teen was assigned an older painter who acted as a supervisor and guardian. All were middle-aged men employed at the plant for years. Those poor guys; it must have been a huge nuisance to oversee a bunch of bumbling, blithe kids in that perilous environment.

For one summer, my partner was Vern. At the time, I thought him old, but he was surely only in his 40s. He was sort of a Tootsie Pop—hard shell on the outside, softer inside. Two memories stand out of my days working beside Vern.

First, he was single-handedly responsible for erasing my phobia of spiders. For more than a week, we had to work in an unused warehouse, replacing the exterior window-panes facing the route of an upcoming bus tour for local VIPs (a pitiable public-relations effort). This building really wasn't abandoned, though. Spiders—many thousands of them—crawled on every surface. Masses scurried across the walls and ceilings. (Picture that scene in the movie "Raiders of the Lost Ark" in which the Well of Souls is filled with snakes; then just replace them with spiders.) Since the floor of this vast warehouse was completely covered with 55-gallon drums, Vern and I were forced to walk atop them to reach the windows we had to replace. Our heads brushed against the spiders on the ceiling. I piled my long hair under my hard-hat, but still fretted about bugs getting caught on an errant lock or falling into the collar of my coveralls.

On the first day of this assignment, I peered into the doorway of that decrepit building, glimpsed those seething hordes of spiders, then froze. Panic surged. My feet went numb. I was rooted to the ground, speechless and quaking. Yet, I knew I'd be mocked by the guys—and likely fired—if I refused to work in there.

Vern saved me. He just started talking, telling me stories and asking about my life. As ever, I couldn't resist the chance to talk, especially about myself. He kept our conversations light and flowing. By engaging me in simple, continuous banter, Vern managed to keep my freaked-out limbic system at bay. I got through the work week, though I'm sure I broke more windows than I repaired because I hammered any spiders that darted onto the panes. Though the warehouse was demolished shortly after that ridiculous vanity tour, my fear of spiders had ended there for good.

My second memory of Vern is something he said as we drove in a company truck to a worksite. He worried about me, he said from out of nowhere, because I was so manipulative. He thought this controlling nature would create sorrow as I got older. The origin of this observation was a mystery to me at the time, but I'm sure it followed on the heels of one of my long-winded tales about a recalcitrant boyfriend. I was shocked and offended. Me, manipulative? Hah, never! Who was he to stick his nose in my business, anyway? Yet, this is the only statement of Vern's I can recall now, decades later. That's how prescient it was. Somehow, he foresaw that I'd waste years and tears trying to control everyone in my life. What he could not predict was that, much later, animal training would become not only my profession, but a means of daily soul work that would help free me from my control-addiction and replace it with something more sustaining.

Vern's observation was my first hint that striving for ever greater power over the actions of others might not be the path to happiness. I easily ignored this insight, of course, and instead spent my 20s honing skills of maneuvering and manipulating, coercing and controlling the people—and later, the animals—around me.

Life has a way of revealing falsehoods, mostly, I believe, through suffering. It causes disillusionment, literally. Illusions get shattered. Two surprising, humiliating and agonizing divorces, one when I was 25 and the other when I was 40, devastated my comfortable routines. Each time, I plummeted into despair. Each time, I felt certain I couldn't survive. I stumbled into the supportive arms of friends and family. I cried through countless hours of therapy. And, sometime between the two break-ups, I began attending church again. Raised

Roman Catholic, I'd stopped going to Mass as soon as I left home for college. But, when I arrived in Tacoma in 1991 to take a job at the Point Defiance Zoo & Aquarium, a co-worker mentioned a different sort of Catholic Church in town. On a whim, I attended Mass at St. Leo Church one Sunday (Pentecost, it turned out). In this wonderful, welcoming Jesuit parish, I found an enduring spiritual home.

The priests and parishioners at St. Leo have been some of my most profound teachers. It's taken only 20 years of their preaching and my praying for me to begin to understand that I really need to get over myself, to detach from my pervasive narcissism and neuroses. For most of my life, my clever—and outsized—ego had kept me believing that I had to be In Charge or else all hell would break loose. It certainly told me I had to be Very Good—no, perfect, actually—to earn the love of others and the love of God. This fueled my imagining all sorts of worthiness hierarchies in which I sorted out which people had, through their good acts, earned the privilege of being loved and which had not. I'd always put my faith in "Thou shall not" rules—rigid attempts at personal perfectionism and the oh-so-subtle coercion and behavioral policing of others. Fortunately, for me and for everybody around me, I've gradually learned to judge a bit less, to breathe a bit more, and to quiet that ego-shout of superiority and separateness.

Over time, I discovered that the miracle of our lives is that God loves us not as a reward for our good behavior, but because it's God's very nature to love. In the words of Fr. Richard Rohr, the brilliant Franciscan priest who runs the Center for Action & Contemplation in Albuquerque, New Mexico, "Divine love is not determined by the worthiness of the object of love but by the Subject, who is always and only Love. God does not love us *if* we change; God loves us so that we *can* change." This unconditional Divine love, for Christians incarnated in Jesus who preached a radical social-order based on grace not merit, now forms the core of my deepest belief.

This spiritual transformation created a dilemma, though. How could I give up being a control freak and still work as an animal trainer and behaviorist? "Unconditional love" is surely not a training plan.

One essential step toward the resolution of this dilemma is to eschew the use of intimidation or physical or psychological pain in the training process. Growing numbers of positive-reinforcement dog trainers have done this, to varying degrees, across the globe for decades. These less coercive methods (e.g., clicker training, lure-reward training, desensitization and classical counter-conditioning) represent a quantum leap forward, in both sophistication and humaneness, from the punitive training techniques espoused by old-fashioned, military-style trainers. Because I'd been a marine-mammal trainer, using these force-free methods and teaching them to my dog-owning students came naturally to me. (Trainers of a vast array of non-dog species have spent little to no time involved in the long-running "reinforce vs. force" debate.)

Yet, over the years, as my spiritual growth continued, I repeatedly found myself struggling with one particular tenet of positive-training philosophy (and, of more old-fashioned training philosophies, too): NILIF. I've come to believe that NILIF contradicts the central miracle I embrace: that I'm surrounded by countless unearned gifts from an extravagantly loving God. So, for me, one of these opposing ideas—"nothing in life is free for dogs" or "grace is abundant for all creatures"—had to go. I just did not realize this until I adopted Nick.

CHAPTER 2

Discord Explored: My Cognitive Dissonance

I reconsidered using Nothing in Life is Free as a foundation for my training programs as the result of several simultaneous events—a personal perfect storm. The first and most salient was when my dog, Nick, bit two of my friends.

Here's some background to put this in context. Nick, a medium-sized herding dog, offspring of generations of mutts, came to live with me unexpectedly. Before I'd met him, Nick had bitten a man (inflicting no injury) and was therefore removed from the service-dog training program in which he'd been enrolled. Talk about failing a temperament test! The program's head trainer requested that I conduct a behavior assessment to ascertain whether it would be safe to re-home Nick. I agreed, and initially met Nick in the restricted environment where he was living (a nearby women's prison). It was immediately evident how frightened he was. He repeatedly snapped and lunged at me; I could not get near enough to touch him.

Despite a prison staff member's comment that Nick was "the most psycho dog I ever saw," I asked the head trainer if I might re-evaluate Nick in a more open setting. The only opportunity to do this was later that week, at 10:30 a.m. on Friday, in a big grassy fenced field between the prison and the vet clinic where Nick had an 11:00 a.m. euthanasia appointment.

As I conducted this second, open-air evaluation, I realized that though Nick was still quite anxious, there was a sound dog somewhere inside. He was, however, literally en route to dying. My astute colleague said, "Your evaluation is terrific news. Now, he needs an experienced foster-home. Where are we going to find that?" Not able to conjure up an alternative, I told her I would take Nick—for two months only. Sixty days, not one day longer. "I'm circling that final day on my calendar," I warned, "and then you'll have to find this dog a permanent home. Can you guarantee Nick will have a home if I rehabilitate him for a couple of months?" She promised he would.

From the start, I resented Nick. Only three weeks earlier, my dear angel dog, a cartoonishly cute, bat-eared old terrier named Gnat, died in my arms of heart failure. He had been my deepest joy, and I wasn't ready to accept another dog into my family, even temporarily. Moreover, I certainly wasn't attracted to Nick. He peed in the house, chewed my books, and cowered and snapped at any man who approached him. His coat was dull and shedding in wads. And forget cuddling; I couldn't even pet Nick. Worst, he guarded his toys and food bowl; he growled whenever anyone came near his treasures. Nick also began to guard me, barking and snarling to keep my other dog, Effie, from getting close.

As soon as Nick moved in with me in January, I began working on his most obvious aggression trigger: men. I took this on as a science project. Nick and I visited public places where men passed at a distance. I called a couple of male friends and asked them to help with the desensitization. I enjoyed seeing the gradual improvement in Nick's behavior. Despite my initial expectations, I found the training fun.

Even more to my surprise, about six weeks into this adventure—in a moment of oxytocin overload—I decided to keep Nick in my family permanently. After a night when I'd been too lazy to tuck Nick into his crate before I went to sleep, he wakened me in bed the next morning by touching the tip of my nose with the tip of his tongue, once, deliberately and delicately. Then he just held my gaze with his soft brown eyes. My heart melted, and Nick transformed from a foster dog into a forever dog.

After several months, I even decided it was safe for Nick to be my demo dog at the group training classes I instructed. I was careful, of course, but I realized there would be ample opportunities in class for me to do counter-conditioning with Nick. As a result of this effort on my "project," Nick showed significant improvements in his behavior. In fact, after about six months, Nick was so thrilled when approached by men that he became goofy and overly effusive in his greetings. He would sidle up to them, wiggly and drooling, looking back to me, expecting steak confetti to rain on his head, as it had hundreds of times previously during our training sessions. Though I had to re-channel his sloppy greeting behavior, this was a vast upgrade over his previous lunging and snapping.

Aggression regression

Today, many years later, Nick is still my dog, truly beloved in ways I neither understand nor question. He has been a magnificent teacher for me. Before Nick, I had worked with about 100 clients who came to me with their aggressive dogs. I knew how to develop behavior-modification programs, how to advise them about treatment and management options. What I had not known was the uniquely mortifying feeling in your gut when your dog bites someone. That mixture of shame, sadness, terror, anger—I'd never felt anything like it. You are simultaneously broken-hearted and furious. Now, when clients say to me, "You don't know what it's like to live with an aggressive dog," I assure them I do.

I felt pretty cocky about our success—until December rolled around. Then I was shocked when Nick—on two separate occasions, both in my living room—bit a friend on the foot. The bites were inhibited; there was no injury either time. Surprisingly, both targets were women. I passed off the first occurrence as a fluke. A few weeks later, however—after the second incident with a different friend—I was distraught. I had no idea what was happening, so I consulted a few dog training colleagues for advice.

I first talked to a trainer whom I deeply respect—a dear long-time friend. She had been a mentor to me, unfailingly generous in giving me piles of expert guidance when I decided I no longer wanted to train big wet animals at the zoo, but dogs. I arrogantly thought that having worked with whales and walruses, I would have an easy time training dogs. She was one of the compassionate people who gently helped me realize that I had more than a bit to learn about dog behavior. Beyond that, she never begrudged me any opportunity to learn about her training techniques, class formats or business structure. So I turned to her for advice about Nick's aggression. What transpired caused ripple effects in my entire approach to dog training.

She suggested that we have lunch at my house and talk about what might be happening with Nick's behavior. This meeting turned out to be quite like an *I Love Lucy* episode. My friend arrived at my front door, a relatively rare occurrence at my house. The screen door was broken, so when Nick jumped on it in his excitement, it opened and bonked my friend on the nose. Not an auspicious beginning. Of course, this was my mistake. Nick should not have had access to the front door. I called him away and was relieved he wasn't barking or snarling. In fact, Nick was happy to see this stranger in our house.

My friend had brought lunch for us. Another kindness. We arranged the food on the coffee table in my living room. Nick was unaccustomed to seeing food on that low table, so it was a tempting novelty. He did what came naturally; he darted his tongue into my soup bowl. His faux pas was surely rude, but not surprising. It was at this point that I started feeling idiotic in front of my esteemed colleague. It never occurred to me, however, that Nick's lack of social niceties was relevant to his aggression. Instead, I thought that Nick was being a nuisance. He wasn't aggressive or dominant; he was revealing his lack of training in house-manners around visitors—100% my responsibility.

As my friend and I sat in the living room to eat lunch and talk about Nick's biting, he jumped onto my big armchair to sit next to me, looking happy, hoping for a share of my food. My colleague was sitting across from us, about to advise me on what I might do to help Nick. It never crossed my mind that jumping on the screen door, licking my soup or leaping onto the chair was pertinent in any way. But I recall her saying, "Right here is your problem. He's spoiled, he has way too much freedom, he should be tethered at your feet right now. Why is he allowed on the chair?"

All I could think was, "What?!" I immediately became defensive, hackles raised. Her question stunned me, so I stammered out some hapless reply while trying to quell my rising irritation. I simply could not accept that this was the root cause of Nick grabbing my visitor's feet with his mouth. In retrospect, I'm sure my friend offered plenty of additional advice, but I wasn't able to hear it.

Of course, my reaction was the result of my illusions shattering. In no way was my friend at fault. In fact, she had given me a huge gift: a change in perspective. What was I upset about anyway? Her comments were exactly the advice I had given to dozens of clients over the years. I'd gone into their homes and given people in my current situation this same analysis. In this experience of advice-receiving rather than advice-giving, however, the whole explanation seemed misguided. I was actually thrilled Nick was in my chair; he was relaxed and not aggressing in any way. While I was feeling proud of him, despite his deficient manners, she was advising that his door-jumping, food-sampling and chair-sitting were fueling his aggression to visitors. It rattled me. More important, it compelled me to ask myself, "Is Nick's lunging and snapping at people correlated with his unearned privileges (e.g., sitting on furniture, sneaking a taste of 'human' food)?" Pretty quickly, I realized that my flood of emotion was not anger at my friend, who was, after all, big-hearted and sincere in her efforts to help us. Instead, I was unnerved because of the sudden realization that I had counseled my own clients with what now seemed to me irrelevant advice.

A short time later, I spoke about Nick's aggression with another colleague—a veterinarian who specializes in behavior consultations. Not knowing the advice I'd already received, she said, "I wonder if you've counter-conditioned Nick to all the possible triggers? Are there stimuli in the situation where he's aggressed that are different than usual?" Together, we analyzed this and discovered several possible factors. Most salient was the fact that on both occasions, my friends had been drinking wine. They weren't drunk, but they'd each had a glass of wine. Nick's inhibited bites happened not when my friends first arrived at my house, but after they'd settled in, had a drink and then stepped over him as he lay nearby. Could a dog perceive the smell of alcohol on a person as a trigger? Before he entered the training program at the prison, Nick had been a stray on city streets. It's conceivable he would have had unpleasant experiences with alcohol-scented people. Until my veterinarian friend pointed it out, I hadn't considered the possibility of olfactory triggers, undetected by humans. Her insight that the alcohol smell might be significant gave me the information I needed to continue and extend Nick's counter-conditioning sessions. Because that training required the participation of friends who smelled like liquor, these rehab sessions were actually quite popular.

This colleague also pointed out that: 1) we had been in the living room on the occasion of both bites, not a place we normally hung out; and 2) the light in the room was dim. Since then, I've noticed in the profiles of some clients' dogs that aggression happens more frequently at dusk or dawn or when the outside light-level is low but the lights inside the house haven't been turned on.

I worked with Nick to change his associations to these triggers, and for the last seven years he's not bitten anyone. What I appreciate most about this process—other than the joy of sharing my life with this now sweet and mostly secure dog—is that it delineated for me two different models for dealing with unwanted, even dangerous, behavior in dogs. One approach is based on controlling access to privileges and freedoms; the other is based on counter-conditioning of triggers and training incompatible replacement behaviors. I realize these need not be mutually exclusive, but they do lead to vastly different entries on a trainer's "To Do" list.

Me-thogram

I was mentally shaken after receiving some of my own standard NILIF advice in a moment of concern and distress. So I decided to do some self-observation and track my interactions with my own dogs. For about a week, I jotted notes about how much of life was "free" for Effie and Nick. In effect, I conducted an informal ethogram (i.e., a quantitative description of an animal's behaviors) on one aspect of my own behavior: how I doled out reinforcers. The result: judged by the tenets of NILIF, I was a huge failure at training my dogs. They got heaps of love from me throughout most days without earning it. Watching myself, I realized that for years I'd been spouting advice to clients that I didn't actually practice.

Maybe, though, my results didn't contradict NILIF because my old dogs are, at this point in their lives, well-behaved. (Note that the definition of "well-behaved" is idiosyncratic and varies widely between dog owners. I use it to mean that their behaviors rarely annoy or worry me. Surely some other people would judge their behavior Not Nearly Good Enough.) Could they have graduated beyond NILIF? Possibly, but if so, we should acknowledge NILIF as a temporary program and develop clear guidelines for judging when it's no longer necessary.

And I'm not off the hook because I'm a professional trainer and animal behaviorist. I don't deserve a "get out of NILIF free" card while my clients, typically "just dog owners" (a pejorative phrase we'd do well to replace), need to follow the rules. That double standard creates a false dichotomy. It implies that I might be able to get away with ignoring NILIF because I know more about training than average dog-owning folks do. But, my knowledge (or lack thereof) is unrelated to "what works to modify dog behavior." Valid training protocols should apply to all dogs, granting that the ease and thoroughness of implementation will vary among owners. It's unfair to say that we (professionals) don't have to follow NILIF, but you (everyone else) do.

Shortly after my brief self-observation study, I shared the results with a long-time colleague—an accomplished and savvy trainer. I told her there'd been a ridiculous amount of me kissing and petting my dogs, and that they often got attention or food without first performing a behavior I requested. She responded with a grin, "Sounds like you've got a new program—fluff love."

Prison jarred

This one is a bit of a tangent, but it occurred during the same time and made me feel the universe was conspiring to spur me to keep reflecting on this concept. It was June 2004, and I heard on the radio a brief news item from the BBC: "The U.S. commander at the center of the Iraqi prisoner scandal says she was told to treat detainees like dogs. Brigadier General Janis Karpinski, who was in charge of the military police unit that ran Abu Ghraib and other prisons, told the BBC she was made a convenient scapegoat for abuse orders by others. She said current Iraqi prisons' chief Major General Geoffrey Miller, who was in charge at Guantanamo Bay, visited her in Baghdad and said, 'At Guantanamo Bay, we learned that the prisoners have to earn every single thing they have. He said they are like dogs and if you allow them to believe at any point that they are more than a dog, you've lost control.'"

This news report is obviously disturbing on many levels, but I was particularly struck by Major General Miller's assumption that the obviously appropriate way to treat dogs—compelled to "earn every single thing they have"—provides a useful model for the best way to treat prisoners. I wondered if the NILIF protocols I'd distributed to students and clients over the years in any way fostered this antiquated notion of how to control dogs and, by extension, anyone whose behavior might cause us problems. This definitely is not the message I want to convey in my work with clients, or in my mission in the larger world. The rigid, coercive relationship a prison guard has with prisoners is the antithesis of the joyful, affectionate, trusting relationship I want to facilitate between people and their dogs. Also, note the implication in Major General Miller's quote that chaos would reign if the prisoners were not strictly controlled in every way and made to earn (in ways unstated) everything.

Shades of grace

The final strand of this braid of experiences that caused me to reject NILIF is the most essential and unavoidable: earned love is antithetical to my deepest beliefs. Love is a gift, a grace superseding reason and beyond the behavioral accounting inherent in all reward-based systems.

This core conviction emerged from the gradual transformation of my heart and mind nurtured by 20 years of homilies delivered by the prophetic and poetic Jesuit priests at my parish. To my amazement, those many years of listening to wise preachers—combined with frequent prayer and participation in SEEL (a nine-month retreat of the

Spiritual Exercises of St. Ignatius Loyola)—revealed the simple truth that worthiness has nothing to do with "deserving" love. My good behavior doesn't turn on God's love; my bad behavior doesn't turn it off. God loves me because it is God's very nature to do so. Here's one more quote from Fr. Richard Rohr: "Whatever God gives is always experienced as totally unearned grace and never as a salary, a reward or a merit badge of any sort. In fact, if you do experience it that way, it is not from God and will not expand your heart, mind or soul." After hundreds of Sunday mornings spent in the fourth pew on the left side, it became impossible for me to maintain the vision of God I'd learned as a kid: the omnipotent and omniscient Being eternally keeping score, noting my every mistake and calculating whether and when I deserved love.

Now, if I fully believe we humans are loved by God "for free"—whether we are good, bad or indifferent—how can I avoid the dissonance that arises from teaching people that their pets must earn love and every other good thing in life?

I tried to get out of this uncomfortable and contradictory place in several ways. First, I decided that this primary principal of unconditional love pertains only to humans. Divine grace must be reserved for humans, and so when we strive to emulate God by manifesting in our lives God's model of indiscriminate love, we need consider only our own species.

For a while, this sounded feasible. But, in reality, it violates everything I've come to understand about the innate dignity and worth of all creatures. Humans may indeed be created in God's image, but we don't have a monopoly on this sacred incarnation of Spirit. I've spent my whole adult life in deep connection with all sorts of animals—dogs and dolphins, whales and walruses—valuing them as evidence of God's immense love for humankind, grateful for their presence as some of my best spiritual directors. If the Creator loves us humans regardless of our behavior, I assume this same grace extends to all creatures.

So my first attempted resolution of the cognitive and spiritual dissonance I was experiencing—this proposed distinction that "love is free" for humans only—felt deeply false.

I tried another way out. You could decide that you'll love your dog unconditionally, but you'll never give him unearned rewards. In other words, you could feel love for your dog on some abstract level, but your actions still could be guided by NILIF. I'm sure this is true for most people. They genuinely love their dogs, but feel they need the rules and structure that NILIF provides.

I find this better in theory than in practice, though. For a while, it provided a good resolution but, in reality, love is actions, not just attitude—a verb more than an idea. Beyond simply having loving intentions, you do things, you demonstrate love, you behave in loving ways. How I feel about my dog—or about anyone (even husbands!)—is nullified if I act in compulsively controlling ways.

Have you encountered situations where withholding love was the best solution? Think of the best relationship you've ever had. Did you keep score? No meaningful relationship is based on "I gave you a gift, so now what are you going to give me in return?" or, "I'm sorry, you didn't earn my smile, my touch, my attention." Deeply satisfying relationships are more emotionally open than that.

The qualities of spontaneity, generosity and the pure joy of being in the presence of an animal can be at loggerheads with NILIF programs. A regimen of strict control of an animal's entire array of reinforcers can come to substitute, quite poorly, for the mutuality and messiness of a real relationship.

In summary, I had these personal incidents with my biting dog, the data obtained by watching my own behavior in relation to my dogs and that troubling quote about the prisoners in Abu Ghraib. I also had my developing faith and the gradual transformation of my own coercive nature, nourished by prayer and liturgy. As a result, I concluded that rationing love and attention—the most basic of reinforcers—cannot be our best approach.

In addition to being a woman of faith striving to be true to my own experience with animals, I'm also a trained scientist and an associate certified applied animal behaviorist. So how does this decision to reject NILIF impact what I now advise my dog-owning clients? I can't tell them to just love their dogs. I have to provide practical solutions to solve their dog-behavior problems.

Before turning our attention to specific alternatives, let's take a look at a few of the herd of sacred cows most of us have grazing in our mental pastures, including two specific examples of reward-rationing programs.

CHAPTER 3
Halving a Cow

In preparation for investigating the usefulness of NILIF programs, let's return to that idea of welcoming some gray into our often black-or-white viewpoints.

Sham-poo

Two years after my adventures with Nick's rehabilitation, I had an epiphany that gave momentum to my new willingness to critically examine "common-sense" beliefs. It involved the killing of a cow—a sacred cow, one of those ideas so essential to daily life that we rarely consider questioning it. What exactly was this obvious truth?

Shampoo. Rinse. Repeat.

At a seminar I presented in upstate New York, a friend and terrific trainer, Parvene Farhoody, said to me during a coffee break, "You're a curly girl." "Hunh? Is that an insult?" I replied. "What does that mean?" She told me about a hair-care program detailed in the terrific book *Curly Girl* by Lorraine Massey. It's a radical way to care for curly hair using no brushes, no combs, no blow dryers and little or no shampoo. I thought, "You've lost your mind. You may be crazy, but I'm washing my hair!" She patiently explained how shampoo damages curly hair and thus began my process of reading, researching and experimenting.

With Parvene's long-distance support, I quickly converted to the Curly Girl program. With few exceptions (mostly at the hands of uncooperative stylists), my hair hasn't been shampooed in five years. It's healthier and better-looking now that I use only water and conditioner. I regretted how much money I'd spent over a lifetime on unnecessary shampoo; I'd bought in to the relentless marketing messages that equate suds with "clean and shiny." Now I go around as a sort of curly-hair ambassador, explaining this unconventional approach to anyone interested. (In Denmark recently, after relating this story as part of a lecture to more than 100 trainers, several asked me to join them for lunch so we could chat—not about dog training, but about their hair.)

Honestly, this weird hair revelation really shook me. It also initiated a new hobby: cow-spotting (or, maybe more appropriately, bull-spotting). I realize that searching out and critically examining sacred cows could easily become a full-time job, but I turned it into a game. What other ideas did I consider obviously true that maybe aren't? What practices did I adopt simply because everyone told me to?

Udder convictions

In just the area of health and wellness alone, I started noticing how many long-held tenets were crumbling under the weight of scientific scrutiny. For example, my eyes popped when I read in Michael Pollan's *In Defense of Food: An Eater's Manifesto* that the lipid hypothesis (i.e., dietary fat is responsible for chronic disease) is not supported by much, if any, evidence. I was stunned. Impossible, I thought. We know, don't we, that dietary fat causes heart disease, cancer and obesity? Apparently not. (See, for example, Gary Taubes' July 2002 New York Times article *"What If It's All Been A Big Fat Lie?"* http://nyti. ms/161Ldv). But, even though my own examination of this heated controversy reveals how tenuous the data are fueling the barrage of marketing that claim low-fat foods are better for us, I cannot yet bring myself to choose a carton of whole milk off the grocery shelf.

One more bit of deflated dogma: sun exposure is bad for your health. Well, this one is obviously true, right? Who hasn't heard the advice to slather high-SPF sunscreen on every exposed inch of your body before going outside? But sunscreen reduces our bodies' ability to make Vitamin D (an SPF 8 sunscreen reduces vitamin-D synthesis by 90 percent) and at least five additional photoproducts we don't get from dietary sources. On his fascinating, certainty-shattering blog, Dr. Michael R. Eades states, "There is no evidence that excess sun exposure causes melanoma, while there is [sic] data showing that chronic sun exposure and vitamin D seem to prevent it." (See his post, *Heliophobe Madness* at http://bit.ly/d3n0C9.) Could we really have gotten it that wrong? Could avoiding sun exposure actually increase our risk of skin cancer?

I'm no medical doctor; please understand I'm not doling out healthcare advice. I'm sharing sincere amazement that my sanguine acceptance of these must-be-true-because-everybody-says-so rules—to avoid eating fatty foods and soaking up sunshine—could be unwarranted.

Hierarchy malarkey

Here's another exceedingly played-out sacred cow: dog owners must be alpha in their family pack, which consists of humans plus dogs. (A veritable Noah's Ark in one sentence!) Let's examine this one in more detail.

In their book *Made to Stick: Why Some Ideas Survive and Others Die*, Chip and Dan Heath detail characteristics that make an idea or explanation "sticky." According to their analysis, stories that are simple, unexpected and concrete capture our imagination and get lodged in our brains. Additional characteristics of sticky ideas, according to the authors, are credibility, emotionality and a basis in story-telling. They offer as ideal cases many urban legends (e.g., if you flash your car's bright lights at a car whose headlights are off, you will be shot by a gang member).

Another perfect example of a sticky story is the ever-popular notion that dogs are essentially domesticated wolves who view their human companions as members of their hierarchical pack. This story is simple (pack structure is presumably a clear-cut linear ranking of alpha, beta and omega animals), unexpected (imagine having descendents of wild wolves right in our living rooms!) and concrete (who hasn't seen TV footage of a wolf pack chasing down a moose or elk?). So sticky is this canine urban-legend that it refuses to die, despite the series of inaccuracies at its core:

1. Wild wolves form hierarchical packs in which individuals vie for dominance. Not always. Maybe not even very often. It turns out this common assumption about the social dynamics of wolves is based on studies of captive animals whose group structure was nonnatural (i.e., the wolves came from various locations and lineages). After a broad review of the scientific literature and thirteen summers spent observing free-living wolves on an island in the Northwest Territories in Canada, wolf ethologist Dr. L. David Mech concluded that social interactions among wolf-pack members are nearly identical to those among members of any other group of related individuals (see Recommended Reading). In essence, the typical wolf pack is a family in which parents guide activities of younger members. Vying for dominance in the pack hierarchy is not a priority. Adult wolves spending their time caring for and teaching younger wolves is.

2. Dogs, close cousins of wolves, also must form packs in which individuals vie for dominance. It is true that there is virtually no difference between the genetic material of dogs and wolves (or between dogs and coyotes). But, from an ecological perspective, dogs and wolves are distinct species because they are adapted to different niches. That is, they earn their livings in different ways. Wolves kill prey, while dogs live in partnership with humans.

Recent studies of the evolution of dogs indicate that this partnership did not occur as a result of our human ancestors' attempts to tame wild wolves to be guard animals or hunting companions. It appears more likely that dogs evolved from a wolf-like ancestor not through artificial selection by humans, but from a process of natural selection filling a new ecological niche. That niche was the town dump, which first appeared approximately 15,000 years ago, at the end of the last Ice Age. This is when humans began creating permanent villages. Wolves found a new food source: they could forage on the waste products in the refuse piles. The individual wolves most able to continue eating even when humans approached were at a reproductive advantage. These less skittish wolves—the tamer ones who didn't flee at the first indication of a nearby human—ate more. Over many generations, this produced the behavioral quality that most distinguishes dogs from wolves: dogs will approach, rather than avoid, humans.

This version of dog evolution, proposed by Dr. Raymond Coppinger and Lorna Coppinger (see Recommended Reading), starring the proto-dog as a scavenger of human waste at village dump sites (think "large rat"), is surely less sexy than proto-dog as noble wolf tamed by clever ancient humans. It's essential for our modern view of dog-training, however, because scavenging "village dogs" don't have a pack structure. They don't hunt cooperatively. Other dogs are competitors in finding edible garbage. So, they live alone, or in groups of two or three.

3. Dogs incorporate humans into their view of pack hierarchies.
Despite data to the contrary, many people still believe dogs form static linear hierarchies of alpha (dominant) and omega (submissive) individuals. Far too many trainers have capitalized on this belief system by arguing that you can solve behavior problems in your dog only when you have established yourself as alpha among the pack of creatures in your home (people and dogs). Legions of dog owners waste valuable time and mental effort complying with spurious rules (e.g., "always eat your meals before your dogs eat theirs"), when instead they could be investing that time and effort conducting simple effective training (e.g., reinforcing desired behaviors). Often, they also use physical force, such as shaking the dog by the scruff of the neck, pinning him on his back, or grabbing his muzzle, because "experts" (on TV, in books, online) say these are methods alpha-ranked wolves use to discipline subordinates.

Even if dogs did form stable linear packs (which, in nearly all cases, they do not), there's no evidence to suggest that dogs perceive humans as part of their species-specific ranking. In general, humans lack the capability to even recognize, let alone replicate, the elegant subtleties of canine body-language. Therefore, it's hard to imagine that dogs ever would consider us as any sort of "pack members."

Here's an alternative sticky story. Dogs are lovable scavengers. Their evolution has made them dependent on humans to provide food. This concept of humans as feeders forms the foundation for a logical, reward-based approach to dog training. Since even wolves organize themselves into family units, we can aspire to be not dominant pack members, but good "parents" instead: loving caretakers and dedicated teachers of our dependent dogs.

Another false moo-ve?

Variants of NILIF abound in the literature, and they range from quite rigid at one end of the spectrum (e.g., "rank reduction" techniques, "doggie boot-camp," "no free lunch") to more flexible and less restrictive at the other end (e.g., "say please" routines, "learn to earn"). Each has somewhat different emphases and ethological grounding, but common elements include:

- The requirement that all of the dog's positive reinforcers (i.e., privileges) are strictly controlled by humans. These reinforcers include, but aren't limited to: food, toys, attention from humans, petting, love, play, access to outside, access to preferred resting areas and access to companions.

- Instructions that all reinforcers be provided to the dog only after the dog has complied with a human's verbal, gestural or body-posture command (i.e., a discriminative stimulus indicating the opportunity for the dog to avoid punishment) or a human's verbal, gestural or body-posture cue (a discriminative stimulus indicating the opportunity for the dog to gain reinforcement). This command or cue is often a signal asking the dog to "Sit."

- Claims that this protocol will teach the dog to accept humans of all ages as leaders.

- Claims by some that, through this approach, humans convey to the dog his place in the family hierarchy (i.e., that he is subordinate to humans).

Example 1

One representative exemplar of this model can be found in an article titled *Nothing in Life is Free* on the website of the Dumb Friends League (www.ddfl.org/sites/default/files/nilif.pdf). Please note that I'm including excerpts from this article not because it's especially egregious, but because it is specific and clearly written, and from a well-respected organization. I encourage you to read the entire document.

> *"Nothing in life is free" is not a magic pill that will solve a specific behavior problem; rather it's a way of living with your dog that will help it behave better because it trusts and accepts you as its leader and is confident knowing its place in your family.*

> ### *How to Practice "Nothing In Life Is Free:"*

> - *Using positive reinforcement methods, teach your dog a few commands and/or tricks. "Sit," "Down" and "Stay" are useful commands and "Shake," "Speak" and "Rollover" are fun tricks to teach your dog.*

> - *Once your dog knows a few commands, you can begin to practice "nothing in life is free." Before you give your dog anything (food, a treat, a walk, a pat on the head) it must first perform one of the commands it has learned…*

> - *Once you've given the command, don't give your dog what it wants until it does what you want. If it refuses to perform the command, walk away, come back a few minutes later and start again. If your dog refuses to obey the command, be patient and remember that eventually it will have to obey your command in order to get what it wants.*

> - *Make sure your dog knows the command well and understands what you want before you begin practicing "nothing in life is free."*

> ### *Why This Technique Works:*
> *Animals that live in groups, like dogs, establish a social structure within the group called a dominance hierarchy. This dominance hierarchy serves to maintain order, reduce conflict and promote cooperation among pack members. In order for your*

home to be a safe and happy place for pets and people, it's best that the humans in the household assume the highest positions in the dominance hierarchy. Practicing "nothing in life is free" effectively and gently communicates to your dog that its position in the hierarchy is subordinate to yours. From your dog's point of view, children also have a place in this hierarchy. Because children are small and can get down on the dog's level to play, dogs often consider them to be playmates, rather than superiors. With the supervision of an adult, it's a good idea to encourage children in the household (aged eight and over) to also practice "nothing in life is free" with your dog.

Example 2

Dr. Karen Overall's popular, seminal and comprehensive reference book, *Clinical Behavioral Medicine for Small Animals,* contains another detailed example in a client handout titled "Protocol for Deference" (pp 410-412). (Note that Dr. Overall never refers to this as "Nothing in Life Is Free.") I include this material because it's cogent and persuasive, because Dr. Overall is an undisputed pioneer in the field of behavior modification for pets and because I distributed this very document to hundreds of my clients over the years. Also, legions of educated behavior consultants have this useful resource on their bookshelf and refer to it regularly.

Here is a very brief excerpt from the "Protocol for Deference." I urge readers to obtain a copy of the book and review Dr. Overall's advice in its entirety:

The intent of this program is to set a baseline of good behavioral interaction between the client and pet and to teach the dog that it must consistently defer to people to receive attention. This is done in a safe, kind, passive manner and is more difficult than clients frequently acknowledge. The reason is as follows: if the clients are talking, reading, or watching television and the dog comes up to them and rubs, paws, or leans against them, the clients usually passively reach out and touch or pet the dog. The dog controlled that entire interaction. Score: dog, 1; human, 0 and the people do not even know that they were conveying any signals other than affection to the dog.

Under no circumstances can the clients touch, love, or otherwise interact with the dog unless the dog defers and awaits their attention. This is done by having the dog sit....

For a dog that already knows how to sit, the only problem is going to be to reinforce this for everything that the dog wants. The rule is: the dog must sit and be quiet to earn anything and everything it wants for the rest of its life. This includes sitting for the following:

- *Food and feeding*
- *Treats*
- *Love*
- *Grooming*
- *Being able to go out–and come in*
- *Having the leash, halter, or harness put on*
- *Having feet toweled*
- *Being invited onto bed or sofa (if desired)*
- *Playing games*
- *Playing with toys*
- *Having a tick removed*
- *Having a wound checked*
- *Being petted or loved*
- *Attention*
- *Anything the dog wants!*

...In fact, unless clients are absolutely willing to exhibit the extensive degree of vigilance recommended here, it is preferable to banish the dog to a place where it can be ignored but not neglected.

Is this the best approach?

As an exercise in cow-spotting, we can ask if the recommendations in these examples are necessary and useful. We can go one step further to ask if they are harmless. Might there be better ways to provide dog owners with a sound foundation for effective behavior modification?

Professional dog trainers often decide—somewhat unconsciously, I suspect—to disseminate NILIF advice to their students and clients, assuming this information is useful and harmless. While I am committed to the benefits of force-free approaches to fostering better behavior in dogs, I'm no longer sure NILIF is benign. I believe there can be significant side effects from implementing these protocols. Because of this, I've changed my own approach to working with clients striving to achieve behavior change in their dogs. By sharing my examination of this issue, I hope to encourage you to reach your own decisions.

CHAPTER 4

Are Alpha Roles Better Than Alpha Rolls? Weaknesses of NILIF

I believe it's long past time that we totally lose all the dominance-based, alpha-obsessed baggage that has infiltrated dog training and acknowledge that successful animal training can be rooted in cooperative partnerships, shared joy and genuine love. It's surprising to me that even progressive (i.e., positive-reinforcement based) trainers often have no qualms about stringent NILIF programs, reasoning that as long as it doesn't advocate physical dominance, then it must be okay.

The whole paradigm of physical dominance needs to go. This includes scruff shakes, forced Sits and Downs, leash corrections and, most iconic of all, alpha rolls. (For those unfamiliar with this ill-advised maneuver, the Monks of New Skete gave these instructions to dog owners: "Grasping the scruff of the dog's neck firmly...shove the dog onto its back with vigor...make eye contact and continue scolding the dog. Keep the dog pinned on its back by applying steady pressure with your hand on its neck." (*How to Be Your Dog's Best Friend*, 1978, p 46.) While most all educated trainers now reject these methods, some seem to be holding onto inherited vestiges of the "humans must reign" mindset. We may now convey this to our dogs kindly, we may do it benignly, avoiding any shoving or yanking, but many trainers still consider it de rigueur that our species calls all the shots. For them, it's still crucial that the trainer is dominant/superior/in control and that the dog is not. In effect, we've gone from alpha rolls to alpha roles: creating relationships with our dogs built on our psychological dominance and rigorous rationing of our attention and affection.

Control vs. communication

NILIF protocols emphasize putting dog owners in control. Granted, a large part of any training program involves controlling the animal's reinforcers. I'm concerned, however, that when we frame dog training in terms of gaining control by never providing the dog any unearned pleasure, we sell ourselves short. Controlling behavior—absent any development of a mutual communication system and reciprocal bonding—can provide illusory and fleeting success. The more permanent and pervasive achievement is teaching dogs how they can make their world work for them by behaving in ways that produce rewards.

There is an addictive and astonishingly joyous pay-off to communicating with animals—connecting with them via a two-way flow of information rather than simply controlling them. We often begin a training program with a new dog by stressing the need for increased behavioral control and its immediate benefits. This may be appropriate, but our narrative—the framework in which we embed our training practices—should lead us to progress naturally beyond this limited perspective.

I was a zookeeper for many years (my actual job title was "staff biologist"). One minor, but real, reason I quit this plum job was because I became so weary of one particular request. I reached the point that if I heard one more zoo patron tell me to "make the whales jump," I thought I'd crack. Of course, I understood the public's desire to get a chance to see these gorgeous creatures perform an athletic feat. But the implication contained in the wording of the request bugged me. It revealed our human fixation with compelling animals to do what we command. These were beluga whales, weighing a ton or more. Exactly how could I "make" any of them jump? I couldn't. But I could ask them. All I or the other marine-mammal trainers ever did was request that the whales jump. They almost always responded immediately and enthusiastically, but not because we were powerful or "in charge." The whales jumped because they had learned to expect to get herring and tongue rubs from their trainers if they did.

We humans repeatedly fall into the trap of thinking that power and control are what successful relationships are about. On deeper reflection, we can see that in our best relationships we communicate easily and clearly—whether with a dog or a whale, or with our best friend or our kids. In the long run, communication trumps control.

Emotional bids

We professional trainers sometimes stop short of discussing the goal of developing two-way communication because our clients don't seem interested. They might say, "I just need our dog to settle down and be quiet." So, we think, "Well, if that's what you want, okay; after all, you're paying me."

Many dog owners actually want more, but don't even know to ask for it. They don't know there could be anything more. Understandably, they usually aren't able to see beyond their immediate frustrations and feelings of powerlessness. I always want to hold out the possibility, though, that the best ultimate goal is to foster communication between owners and dogs. To facilitate this, I simply cannot suggest that all interactions be so regimented that the client is forbidden from responding to her dog's gentle request for attention (e.g., a slow approach followed by soft, prolonged eye contact) with, "Hi there" and a kiss on the nose. This spontaneous moment of affection violates NILIF because the owner "gives in" to the dog's attention-seeking without asking the dog to "Sit" first. But this seemingly trivial exchange, this bit of bonding, is a vital component of communicating in an emotionally open and honest way.

Of great relevance here is the work of Dr. John Gottman, professor emeritus of psychology at the University of Washington and co-founder, along with his wife, Dr. Julie Schwartz Gottman, of the Gottman Relationship Institute (see Recommending Reading). For more than 30 years, Dr. John Gottman has studied what makes marriages last and what makes them fall apart. He is famous for devising a technique which predicts with higher than 90% accuracy the success or failure of a relationship over the subsequent three years by documenting each person's physiology and behavior during a challenging conversation and by interviewing them about their past.

One crucial finding: satisfied couples maintained a five-to-one ratio of positive-to-negative interactions in their relationship. In couples heading for divorce, that ratio slipped to less than one-to-one.

Through his analyses of the videotaped conversations of thousands of couples, Dr. Gottman has also concluded that "emotional bids" are an essential concept:

> *These bids can be a question, a look, an affectionate touch on the arm or any single expression that says, "I want to feel connected to you," [Gottman] says. A response to a bid can be a turn toward, away or against someone's request for emotional connection... Gottman says people don't get married, make friends, or try to maintain ties with siblings to have those relationships fail. Yet many fail because people don't pay enough attention to the emotional needs of others. For example, research from his apartment lab showed that husbands who eventually were divorced ignored the bids from their wives 82 percent of the time compared to 19 percent for men in stable marriages. Women who later divorced ignored their husband's bids 50 percent of the time while those who remained married disregarded only 14 percent of their husband's bids.... The system of bids and turns and emotional command systems works broadly across all kinds of relationships, not only marriage, according to Gottman. And opportunities for making and responding to bids abound. A typical happy couple may make 100 bids over the course of the dinner hour.... "A relationship is about these small moments, these bids and responses. It is the way intimacy and trust are built." [Joel Schwarz; http://depts.washington. edu/uweek/archives/2001.05.MAY_10/_article11.html]*

People in relationships repeatedly make emotional bids to one another—for affection, attention, assistance and information. For example, a wife, trying to get her husband's attention for a conversation, may say, "Hey, did you hear about the new restaurant that just opened?," If her husband keeps typing on his laptop, ignoring her, he's turning away her bid for attention. If he says, "Can't you see I'm busy?" he's turning against her bid. If he replies, "Oh really?" and lifts his eyes from the computer, he's turning toward her.

I believe it's reasonable to extrapolate this concept to gain potential insights into our relationships with any significant other, including our dogs. It suggests there is a considerable price to pay for snubbing (i.e., dismissing, turning away, or frustrating the expectations of) or stonewalling (i.e., withdrawing or being emotionally or physically unreachable) them. Yet NILIF protocols state that whenever a dog solicits our attention, we are to ask the dog to "Sit" (or perform another known behavior). If the dog does not respond correctly, we are to walk away, assured that sooner or later the dog will have to obey us/acquiesce.

You can dismiss this contradiction by deciding that the research into successful human relationships is irrelevant to our discussion of dog training. Belief in the spurious concept of lupomorphism (the attribution of wolf traits and behavior to dogs) could fuel such rejection of Gottman's (and other psychologists') data. After all, this tired refrain drones, dogs are basically pack animals with a linear dominance hierarchy and therefore have not evolved the capacities to participate in any sort of power-sharing relationship with us humans. It follows, then, that they must always be subordinate/deferent/lower on the totem pole.

I believe the data about emotional bids reveal a core truth about all meaningful relationships between animals who experience emotions. This includes us humans, of course, and dogs too. I've not lost sight that dogs are different than people. Nor do I think that our relationships with dogs perfectly parallel the relationships we build within our own species. But it seems unwise to ignore the deleterious effects of routinely turning away from our dogs' bids for attention or assistance. In our zeal to ensure that we never encourage—intentionally or inadvertently—demanding or bratty behavior from our "status-seeking" dogs, we may have enshrined, in NILIF, a recipe for human passive-aggressiveness.

Hidden under a veneer of alleged cooperation, passive-aggressive behavior habitually frustrates the wishes of others. I always think of passive-aggression as the extreme version of the negative-punishment quadrant of the operant conditioning grid, whereas typical (i.e., "non-passive") aggression is the extreme version of positive punishment. (This presumes that these aggressive responses are contingent on behavior by the person or animal being punished. Otherwise, the aggression isn't even a consequence, in the behavior-analytical sense of the word.)

Years ago, I read an article in the *Seattle Times* newspaper titled "He's a BAD Dog!" In it, the reporter, Shirleen Holt, describes her futile attempts to resolve her Jack Russell Terrier's "evil" disobedience. She catalogs a litany of complaints about Kiley's behaviors and gives a chronology of training approaches she tried. Referring to advice she received from "an animal behaviorist," Ms. Holt writes:

> *I tried her suggestions, which included a passive-aggressive form of training called 'earned petting.' That is, I was to ignore his demands for attention and acts of defiance and communicate with him only on my terms, rewarding him with affection when he responded to one of my commands.*

She goes on to say that she failed on the first night because Kiley grabbed a stick of butter off the table and so she had to chase him or else, "that butter would end up on my carpet one way or another." (One wonders why Kiley had access to the butter; I suspect that behaviorist also might have counseled Ms. Holt about temporary management tools such as tethers or exercise pens.)

The article concludes by describing a phone conversation Ms. Holt had with Mathilde DeCagney, the trainer of Moose, the Jack Russell Terrier who played Eddie on the TV show *Frasier*.

> *[Kiley] has nothing wrong with him," she said, her French accent softening the sharp words. "It's all you." I winced, but I knew she was right. She listed the reasons: Kiley is a working dog without a job; he's a social dog without enough companionship; he's a smart dog without enough mental stimulation; and he's a hyper dog without enough exercise.*

In other words, Kiley has needs! Like all dogs, he has legitimate physical and psychological needs. Advice from a trainer or behaviorist that the owner should institute NILIF, absent any acknowledgment and plan to fulfill these needs, creates the likelihood that both owner and dog will be miserably frustrated.

Behavior matters

Have you ever noticed how much pleasure people get from asking an animal to do a behavior, and then seeing the animal respond, immediately and correctly? Whether it's a child asking a neighbor's dog to give a High Five, a man on a behind-the-scenes tour at the oceanarium asking a dolphin to perform a backflip or a girl proudly showing her friends how her cat will meow on cue—in all these cases, it's satisfying to experience our words or gestures eliciting the intended behavioral response. We signaled our request and the environment (the animal) complied. Our action "worked." It felt good.

Social psychologists refer to our perception of this linkage between our behavior and the subsequent reinforcing event as an internal locus of control. Individuals with a high internal locus of control believe that events result primarily from their own actions; in other words, their behavior matters. Individuals with a high external locus of control believe that forces outside their influence (e.g., other individuals, chance, etc.) primarily determine events.

According to Steven R. Lindsay, dog behavior consultant and author:

> *The NILIF program...is embedded into every significant social transaction for the remainder of the dog's life so that family members can dictate control over the dog's 'daily decisions.' The NILIF process...appears intended to externalize the locus of control and thereby undermine the dog's ability to initiate independent actions in search of reward. As such, the program appears to promote an increasing social dependency and powerlessness, whereby the owner dictates what the dog can do and when it can do it while frustrating the dog's ability to produce social rewards on its own initiative. (p. 384; see Recommended Reading.)*

This is diametrically opposite to my goals in training. Encouraging animals to engage with their environments, to have initiative, to move and to try different behaviors—these are at the very heart of clicker training. (More on this in Chapter 5.) Through systematic training, I strive to teach dogs to make appropriate "daily decisions," often independent of—though not in opposition to—their owners' dictates, thereby producing all sorts of rewards for themselves.

Dr. Susan Friedman, research assistant professor of psychology at Utah State University, pioneer in the application of Applied Behavior Analysis (ABA) to parrots and other companion animals and a personal hero of mine, sums it up eloquently:

> The degree to which a behavior reduction procedure preserves learner control is essential to developing a standard of humane, effective practice. Research demonstrates that to the greatest extent possible all animals should be empowered to use their behavior to control significant events in their lives, i.e., to use their behavior effectively to accomplish a desired outcome. Indeed, that is what behavior has evolved to do. (From "What's wrong with this picture? Effectiveness is not enough." See Recommended Reading.)

If all you have is a hammer, all problems look like nails

I decided a couple of years ago to stop subscribing to online chat lists where professional trainers discuss dog behavior because, among other reasons, I couldn't bear to read one more example of NILIF advice doled out to someone whose puppy peed in the house or whose dog got car-sick or jumped on the furniture. Recommendations to institute NILIF were ubiquitous; it was an idea as sticky and common as duct tape. It was also, for some "experts," a panacea. Many trainers prescribed it liberally, figuring, I suppose, that like sugar pills it can't hurt and it might even help.

On the other extreme, it was common to read NILIF protocols recommended as a stand-alone cure-all for seriously aggressive dogs. The implication was that if an owner could adhere to the NILIF regimen, the aggression would be "cured." Any reoccurrence of the aggressive behaviors could then be attributed to the owner's non-compliance. This view is, to me, naïve, inaccurate, dangerous and, in some cases, misogynistic. I have worked with many female clients who had been told by a previous trainer that if they could just "develop some backbone" and stop being such a softy, the dog would stop lunging/snapping/biting at people/dogs/cats/bicycles.

After reading this book, even if you decide to continue using and recommending NILIF protocols, I hope you'll reflect on what sorts of behavior problems they might address. Do you believe they are appropriate for every possible concern a dog owner may have? How about noise sensitivities? Forging instead of heeling? Fence-fighting with the neighbor dog? Dropping the dumbbell on the retrieve? Entering the weave poles wrong? Separation anxiety?

Nothing is free? Really?

Years ago, I trained dolphins to detect and disable deep-moored mines in the open ocean. One day, a co-worker—a long-time "old-school" trainer—decided he would use a creative method to motivate the bottlenosed dolphin assigned to him to beach from her home pen into the small motorboat (a 21-foot Boston Whaler) used to transport animals to the open-ocean training areas.

The dolphins sometimes were unable to swim alongside our boats—the cetacean version of "heeling"—to the worksites located in the deeper waters of Kaneohe Bay because it took too long. Instead, we'd ask them to beach (i.e., part-leap and part-slide) onto a huge triangular "transport pad" that we'd hang out the port side of the custom-designed boat. The thick blue pad would jut over the edge of the dolphin's home pen, and the trainer would kneel on top, near that edge, and then signal, with a palm slap on the pad, the dolphin to "hop in." Once the dolphin chose to do so, we might give her a mouthful of fish and push her back into the pen (a vitally important "fake" trial). Or else two trainers would lift the fluke-end of the pad with the dolphin inside, rotating it 90 degrees counter-clockwise onto the stern of the boat. There the dolphin would ride for 5 to 50 minutes, kept wet and cool by a trainer on board.

Beaching onto a boat obviously isn't a natural behavior for a dolphin, so it was a high priority for the trainers. We worked on it often, attempting to get a fluent and reliable response from each dolphin every time we slapped that transport pad. If a dolphin chose not to beach onto the boat (i.e., not to go out in the ocean to work), there could be no further training that day.

This older trainer had figured out that the way to "encourage" his uncooperative dolphin to jump into the boat was to place a blue plastic tarp over the entire surface of her rectangular pier-side pen, blocking all access to air. The only way his dolphin would have been able to breathe was by getting out from under that suffocating tarp by beaching into the boat adjacent to the pen. In quickly mounting horror, I watched this scenario develop. As soon as I realized what he was setting up, I raced to fetch the on-site veterinarian, who interceded immediately. The dolphin was unharmed.

When this particular trainer implemented NILIF, he pushed it to its supposedly logical—but truly insane—limit: you have to earn your next breath. I spoke to him many days later about his plan; he sincerely thought it was a clever way to motivate his dolphin.

Another example: I used to work at a veterinary hospital. For a while, part of my job was managing its extensive boarding kennels. I remember the controversy generated when I refused admittance to a guide dog in training. This was not a popular decision, to be sure, but this dog's handler insisted that we not provide any "free" water in the kennel run. The protocol for this dog—in training to be a guide for a blind person—dictated that the dog must earn every sip of water. When I questioned the appropriateness of this, the dog's handler responded, "Oh, absolutely. Free water is the first step toward creating a spoiled dog."

Despite how extreme these two examples seem, never forget that plenty of people take advice literally. Many will attempt to follow any instructions doled out by a professional trainer, without first applying filters questioning whether it could be dangerous, cruel or foolhardy. So, if you advocate NILIF, what exactly do you mean? Is it really **nothing** is free?

Maybe you responded to these examples by thinking, "Of course reasonable people don't include air and water in the list of rationed rewards." (Note that both the people in these examples were experienced professional trainers.) What other "privileges," then, aren't included in your NILIF protocol? What additional things are so obviously necessities of life that they really should be free? My list would include, at least: love, safety, air, water, minimal daily calories, time to rest and companionship.

This doesn't mean you never can use these things as reinforcements for your dog's good behavior. For example, let's say I notice that, at the end of a long walk, my dog Effie is thirsty. As I load her into my car, another dog happens to pass us. Before Effie possibly responds by barking, I can mark (with a verbal "Yes!") the moment she glances at that dog, and then I can offer her a bowl of water. In this case, I found a way to provide Effie with water, contingent on behavior I like. I caught her doing something desired (by me) and, as a consequence, I gave her something desired (by her). Despite my using water as a handy reinforcer in this instance, Effie typically has access to fresh water at all times. And, if she had barked at that dog before I could respond, I would have waited a minute before giving her the water "for free."

Eat no fat

Remember that story about the Navy dolphins riding aboard the Boston Whalers? I mentioned that it took two trainers, one on either side of the triangular peaked transport pad with a bottlenosed dolphin inside, to lift the fluke-end onto the stern of the boat. This was no easy feat; these dolphins could weigh nearly a half-ton.

When the Naval Oceans System Center (NOSC) hired me in 1988, I was one of only three female trainers—all new employees—on the "applied side" of the Navy's dolphin research facility at the Kaneohe Marine Corps Air Station on Oahu. Some of the well-established male trainers were not eager to share their worksite with us women, and the hazing Kathi and Debbie and I endured was rather remarkable.

One of the more clever ploys to get us to quit was to assert that there was no way that two women ever could lift a big ol' dolphin onto the work-boat without the aid of a man. Because an open-ocean training team consisted of one trainer, one boat driver and one dolphin, it was indeed possible that Kathi and I—as co-workers on the same training session—might be the sole people on a boat. We might, therefore, be required to lift a transport pad containing Haole, the heaviest of our project's ten dolphins—a half Atlantic-bottlenosed/ half Pacific-bottlenosed hulk weighing just under 1000 pounds.

Rather than concede, Kathi and I requested some time to prepare for the physical test of lifting Haole on board. Our boss agreed to let us try. Kathi and I began going to the gym on the military base most mornings before work. The Marines there initially looked at us scrawny women—each weighing no more than 120 pounds— as a joke. But most ended up either ignoring us or supporting our crazy quest. We made friends and gained work-out advisors. To my surprise, I discovered that I really enjoyed lifting weights. And Kathi and I triumphantly passed our "Haole-lifting" test about two months later.

During this time, one bit of advice I got from my brawny weight-lifting partner, Lee, was, "don't eat any fat." He was serious, even going so far as to check my lunch cooler to see if the yogurt or cheese had even a gram of fat lurking within. I clearly remember trying to avoid all fat in my diet and failing, over and over. It was a goal I just couldn't attain. (Nor, as I now realize, should I ever have tried. Fat is an essential part of a healthful diet.)

In a similar way, NILIF is also an unyielding regimen, requiring us to excise a necessary, healthy part of a normal relationship. This impossible standard guarantees that the dog owner will fail, likely resulting in feelings of guilt and incompetence. Nobody can actually do it, except maybe a dedicated control freak. (Like me. Sort of. Actually, I'm in recovery. There really should be a 12-Step program for this.) And I'm betting that any training procedure that shapes the trainer into being a compulsive micro-manager is not a good thing. In fact, striving to perfectly regulate the flow of love and reciprocity in a relationship is the opposite of enlightenment.

I still remember chatting about this idea with a client, Deb, in her kitchen years ago. A visiting friend of hers overheard our conversation, and then told me about a ritual her family invented. First thing every morning, each person and pet gathers on the parents' bed. This includes mom, dad, two young kids and two Dachshunds. They then proceed with "Everybody Loves Everybody." This means that each family member kisses every other person and each dog while saying, "I love you." They'd been doing this for years. As I pictured this scene of early morning connection and chaos, I felt tears well up. (Still do.) I couldn't imagine a more blessed start to a day. The friend then said to me, "So, would this NILIF thing put a stop to this? If so, it's crazy."

If you realize that dog owners actually aren't going to have their dog Sit for every good thing, don't tell them to do it. When they can't accomplish this unrealistic goal, and their dog subsequently behaves badly, they'll blame themselves. "Well, I didn't do what the trainer said—I petted Spot when he walked up to me without asking him to Sit first. So my breaking the rules caused her barking/lunging/nipping/jumping/peeing/escaping."

Clients, guilt-stricken and confessional, have said to me, "I pet my dog sometimes when he asks for it." They act like they're in trouble for doing something completely natural and caring. In many cases, my clients have dogs with serious behavior problems, so the next sentence out of their mouth might be, "So I'm responsible for him biting." They believe it's their indulgence— their giving in to petting or play—that's caused their dog to bite.

Don't we trainers sometimes fan that feeling? Heck, I've actually said to people, "If you don't control everything, you're going to have dire consequences." In trying to ensure we don't end up with bratty dogs, we've swung the pendulum all the way to the other side by saying, "Humans must control every interaction."

Note one more thing about owners who try instituting NILIF but can't manage to ensure that every member of the family is 100% successful in following the protocol: they're actually setting up a schedule of intermittent reinforcement of the dog's "bad" (i.e., demanding, attention-seeking) behaviors. If they or their spouse or their children occasionally skip the rule that the dog must Sit before every privilege or interaction, the dog will be intermittently reinforced for attempts at "direct access" of rewards, often at times that the dog is being most insistent (i.e., pushy). This is likely to make these behaviors even more resistant to extinction, ensuring they will remain in the dog's repertoire for a very long time.

What about Pavlov?

NILIF programs contradict training procedures that employ classical counter-conditioning (i.e., Pavlovian conditioning). When I explain classical counter-conditioning to my clients, it's challenging to convince them that they should feed (or play with) their dog every time that the dog's environmental trigger appears, despite what the dog is doing at that moment. I tell them we are going to "open the bar"— Jean Donaldson's evocative term for providing behaviorally non-contingent largesse—whenever the dog sees, hears, feels or smells the thing he considers spooky (i.e., the trigger). The dog doesn't earn this bounty by sitting or looking at his handler or otherwise deferring. Instead, the food or play is contingent on the trigger appearing to the dog, not on the dog's operant behaviors.

When I initially conducted classical counter-conditioning trials with Nick, I fed him steak every time he noticed an unfamiliar man nearby, regardless of what Nick was doing. Of course, I tried to arrange our early training scenarios so that these men didn't get too close; I tried to avoid provoking a full-blown aggressive response by Nick. There were plenty of times when I fed Nick as he was tense or beginning to snarl. To get the steak, Nick didn't have to obey my command, defer to me or even be "good." This is because in classical counter-conditioning, it is the trigger, not the dog's good behavior, which "makes" the food happen.

How can this be consistent with NILIF protocols? It presents quite a dilemma if you've first convinced clients to adhere to NILIF and then you say, "Now, we're going to do this counter-conditioning procedure, so I want you to toss liver to Bailey whenever he notices a bicycle going by." The client is likely to say, "Wait, doesn't he have to earn that liver? Doesn't he have to look at me, or sit or nose-touch my hand first?" "No, no, no," you reply, "not in *this* procedure." The client then says, or at least thinks, "What?!"

NILIF also contradicts another foundational training technique: capturing. More about this in Chapter 5.

Chains aren't the answer

Here's another problem. Consider this situation. Your dog approaches you while you're sitting on the couch, trying to read a book. He nudges your arm or sticks a toy in your lap. What would NILIF advise? Ask the dog to "Sit" and then pet him or throw the toy if you want to. Just make sure you require him to "Sit" first. Have the dog defer or "say please": let him earn the petting or play.

But this doesn't discourage the initial attention-seeking behavior at all. It just creates a behavior chain. When your dog attempts to initiate an interaction with you, if you then ask her to do a behavior you've repeatedly rewarded her for doing in the past, you've actually reinforced her initial nudging, pawing or barking (i.e., attention seeking).

The only non-punitive way behavior chains are broken is by inserting a pause. There has to be a brief time gap: ten or twenty seconds (or longer) of no interaction with the dog. It won't work if your dog, by her behavior, says, "Pet me, pet me, pet me!" and you respond with, "Okay, but only if you 'Sit' first." You didn't gain any future behavioral improvement—any lessening of the dog's initial attention-seeking—except that now you've got sitting mixed into it all.

Another example: your dog is pawing at the kitchen door to go outside. Paw, paw, paw. You walk up and say, "Okay, but first you have to 'Sit.'" You'll feel better about this routine because your dog will be "polite" before you let him out. You didn't decrease the likelihood of future pawing, however. In fact, you actually locked pawing into that behavioral sequence.

The behavior chain = Bailey does a behavior you'd rather he didn't → you then "redirect" him to do a polite/obedient/deferential behavior, such as "Sit" → he complies → you provide him with whatever he was asking for in the first place.

It may seem reasonable to hope that the dog will eventually skip the beginning of this flowchart, opting just to Sit to get you to open the door or pat his head. But operant conditioning doesn't work that way. Your immediate "redirection" to a known, previously reinforced behavior ensures that the initial misbehavior gets reinforced, that is, made more likely.

When working with extremely challenging dogs, I'm occasionally tempted to distill my training advice to, "Reward any behaviors the dog does except the three you consider most annoying." For example, an owner might decide that his personal "Most Obnoxious List" for his dog includes whining, furniture-chewing and pawing people's legs. If we arranged things so that his dog's daily pleasures were contingent on **any** behaviors other than these—even mediocre or imperfect behaviors—while also ignoring and/or preventing these three, we'd likely see a significant shift in the dog's repertoire. Lacking "fuel," those worst behaviors would become less likely over time. We could then revise the list, deciding what the next most annoying behaviors are, and applying the same extinguishing strategy to these. What's notable in this approach is that we are freeing the owner to interact with his dog in any way that doesn't reward obnoxiousness (as operationally defined by the owner). Ironically, asking a dog to "Sit" immediately after he does any of these "bottom three" behaviors does, in fact, reinforce it.

Occam's Razor

I realize that the behavioral outcomes from adhering to the precepts of NILIF might be beneficial in some cases. If NILIF programs inspire a dog owner to start controlling reinforcers and intentionally giving them to a dog at appropriate times, then it's quite likely there will be a measurable improvement in the dog's behavior. But there are other ways to inspire similar behavioral change in our clients and students that don't resort to, "the dog must earn every privilege." You could get the necessary information across in a more flexible—and, frankly, boring—way: "Reinforce behaviors you like, prevent reinforcement of behaviors you don't like."

This prescription is not as simple or as visually evocative as NILIF, but it's more parsimonious. "Occam's Razor" says that the simplest explanation is the best; you shouldn't add hypothetical constructs to something that can be explained more simply. So you can get your clients and students behaving in ways that provide their dogs with more contingent reinforcers for desired behaviors without saying, "You must never give anything away for free or else your dog will see you as not assertive, not the leader, and you're headed for anarchy." Where can spontaneous joy bubble up in such a relationship? I live with dogs because they make me irrationally happy. I glow when I'm near my dogs and often feel bursts of bliss just looking at them. When we're reunited after an absence of a day or longer, I'm as excited as a toddler on Christmas morn. I admit that I'm skeptical that people can readily develop this sort of free-flowing, life-affirming, soul-nourishing connection with their dogs if they are scrupulously monitoring the possible unearned reward inherent in every interaction.

It's not that the behavioral outcome (for the dogs, at least) of NILIF is inevitably negative. Instead, it's about how we tell our story—what we choose as our narrative framework for talking to students and clients. We have the privilege of educating dog owners, and we need to choose carefully how we explain the foundation of our behavioral advice. Words matter. We surely need to help our students change their dogs' behaviors. And, in most cases, the majority of positive-reinforcement-based trainers agree to a large degree about what we'd ask our students to do. But how do we convey our message?

I'm going to present alternatives to saying, "In order to have a safe, happy household and a good relationship with your dog, he can never get any privileges without performing a human-requested behavior to earn it." I suggest our new paradigm could be about exchanging reinforcers: your dog gives you reinforcers (in the form of good behavior) and you give reinforcers to your dog, back-and-forth in a continuous flow. I can use this approach to help create positive behavioral changes in my clients and their dogs while at the same time fostering reciprocity and the formation of the deepest bonds of affection.

CHAPTER 5

If Not NILIF...?

I began this book by stating that animal training is an inherently manipulative endeavor. We train animals to bring some order to the behavioral bedlam that can result from a lack of intentional training—an "anything goes" mentality—good for neither the dog nor the people living with the dog. In seeking alternatives to the NILIF framework, we need not throw out the baby—consistent and effective training—with the bathwater—the side effects of broad-scale rationing of the dog's access to "good things." Could we create one or more sticky stories that surpass the advantages of NILIF and provide an alternate framework for sound and successful dog training?

Michael Pollan, in his 2008 bestseller *In Defense of Food: An Eater's Manifesto,* suggests a compact maxim for deciding how we humans can best feed ourselves: "Eat food. Not too much. Mostly plants." It's his essential message, summarizing a comprehensive and far-reaching examination of the Western diet and its effects on our health and culture. He pulls out the core, so to speak, and conveys enough in this significant little statement that it could change a person's behavior forever.

Can we formulate an equally concise statement to convey the core of effective and humane dog training? Stripped down to a mantra that would fit on a bumper sticker—a literally sticky idea—we could say, "Reinforce behaviors you like; prevent reinforcement for behaviors you dislike." (Note that this statement is proactive and differs from the more reactive, "Reinforce behaviors you like; *remove* reinforcement for behaviors you dislike.") This is behaviorism encapsulated. It's powerful and profound.

But is it sticky? Remember the key characteristics sticky ideas tend to have in common, according to Chip and Dan Heath in *Made to Stick:* they are simple, unexpected, concrete, credible and emotional. They also tell a story. "Reinforce behaviors you like; prevent reinforcement for behaviors you dislike" is simple, for sure, and because it's distilled from decades of laboratory research around the world, it's credible. Yet it's surely not sticky. There's no narrative. It's abstract, not concrete, and I challenge you to find a shred of emotionality in it.

Let's see if we can embellish the bumper-sticker version of behaviorism enough to make it memorable and useful for both dog owners and professional trainers.

Alternative 1: SMART x 50

Have you heard the fitness advice which states that the key to weight loss and better health is to walk 10,000 steps each day? This idea originally was popularized in Japan. According to Dr. Yoshiro Hatano, a professor at Kyushu University of Health and Welfare, seven million pedometers are sold annually in his country. Health experts may disagree on the exact number of steps that result in noticeable fitness gains, but "walk 10,000 steps each day" provides guidance that is simple and concrete (literally, if sidewalks are involved).

Adapting this "counting directive" for dog training, we could advise, "Positively reinforce your dog's good behaviors fifty times each day." Not bad, but it's too technical. Instead, how about, "Fifty times each day, reward your dog when he's doing something useful or cute?" This is better; it's concrete and simple.

But is it too simple? Professional trainers will immediately think of the ways this protocol falls short: it doesn't provide details on how to reward the dog or who should reward the dog, it doesn't define what "useful" or "cute" behaviors are, it doesn't say what to do about unwanted behaviors, etc.

Just as the person walking 10,000 steps per day must augment that core advice with additional health considerations (e.g., not smoking, limiting caloric intake, getting enough sleep), the dog owner following the "fifty rewards per day" guideline will need to bolster this by attending to further details. So many benefits result from instilling into dog owners' daily routines this habit of reward, however, that it can serve as clear and helpful foundational advice.

We could envision that a significant portion of the good behaviors we want to develop are already in our dogs. By saying "yes" to these, over and over, we encourage our dogs' cooperative, calm, controlled actions. Our frequent, precisely timed, meaningful reinforcements— our "yeses," each followed by an event the dog considers rewarding— will etch desirable behavioral grooves into our dogs' repertoires.

Cultivating good behaviors in dogs

This emphasis on nurturing good behaviors through reinforcement is analogous to an organic approach to cultivating a healthy landscape. Organic gardeners spend plenty of time tilling the soil, enriching it with compost and other nutrients. They choose fruits and flowers appropriate for their soil and light conditions. They welcome a diversity of plants, bugs and birds, and are open to being pleasantly surprised by the occasional volunteer that sprouts in their beds.

From the start, positive-reinforcement trainers devote time to developing a fertile, rich rapport with our animals. We build trust, the tilth of relationships. We commit to the dictum, "First, do no harm." We acknowledge the potential for irrevocable fall-out resulting from widespread use of positive punishment, the Roundup™ in a trainer's wheelbarrow. We also value diversity and are grateful for the myriad behaviors our animals offer because we realize that behavioral variability is essential to efficient training. When unwanted, weedy behaviors crop up in our animals, we understand that the best way to get rid of them is to nurture desirable substitutes. And we know that just as weeds take advantage of sterile, microorganism-depleted lawns, undesirable habits (e.g., destructiveness or whining) require a behavioral void to take root.

Cultivating good behaviors in trainers

I expand on this "fifty rewards a day" protocol by giving my clients information about how to be successful behavior engineers. I suggest that they "Get SMART"—that is, that they practice "See, Mark And Reward Training." Those three components—seeing good behavior, marking good behavior (often with a click or a "yes") and rewarding good behavior—are the core competencies of successful trainers. This trio of skills comprises the technique called "capturing" (or "scanning" by some marine-mammal trainers): capitalizing on the numerous desirable behaviors an animal performs over the course of an average day by: 1) noticing them, 2) pointing them out to the animal, and 3) then giving the animal a reward in order to increase the strength of those behaviors. We make efforts to reinforce behaviors we like so those behaviors become more frequent, more intense and longer.

At first, it's difficult to appreciate the power of Seeing, Marking and Rewarding. It seems as if the trainer is being passive. What about commanding or cueing the dog to do something? Where is the talking, prompting and luring common in many training procedures? These forms of trainer input all have their place, of course, but are not a primary part of SMART. In SMART, the trainer isn't "doing nothing," but is instead allocating mental resources to the most critical activity of all: paying attention to what the dog is actually doing and thereby truly seeing behavior. (Note: The "S" should actually stand for "sensing" because visually-impaired people can be fabulous trainers, using sensory systems other than vision to perceive their animals' good behavior.)

SMART is easy to do and it works far better than seems possible to novices. How naïve it sounds to say that paying attention to good behavior and exchanging food (and other rewards) for it will create long-lasting, reliable changes. But a simple, week-long experiment will demonstrate the power of this approach. Choose a desirable movement—serious or silly—your dog makes. Two possibilities are: 1) lying down, or 2) lowering the chest to the ground in a bowing motion, while the back legs remain straight. Use a click (or some alternate acoustic marker such as the spoken word "yes," or a thumbs-up gesture if your dog is deaf) to indicate the exact instant your dog does this behavior (i.e., moves floorwards). Follow each mark by giving your dog a tiny piece of food. You can throw the treat on the ground, hand it to your dog or toss it for him to catch. Over the course of the week, you should notice your dog's behavior change as a result of your marking and feeding—that is, your reinforcement of the chosen behavior. You will see the frequency of that behavior increase. Your dog should be lying down, or bowing, or whatever you chose, more often. This means you are well on your way to having an obedience behavior or a trick on cue, ready to "fire" when you ask for it.

Because it's so effective (i.e., reinforcing for the trainer), SMART can easily become a habit for dog owners who try it for a couple of weeks. Pretty quickly, it becomes difficult to imagine NOT doing it. Yet, Seeing, Marking and Rewarding voluntary behaviors violates versions of NILIF that require trainers to ask their dog to respond to a command (or to a trainer-produced cue) before the dog receives any rewards. SMART frees us to reward dogs any time they aren't annoying or worrying us. The more we do this, the more our dogs will behave in ways that please us and the less risk we'll have of accidentally reinforcing them for pushiness.

This very minute, my two dogs are sleeping in my office, Effie with her head hanging off a huge fleece dog-bed and Nick curled tightly on the couch next to me. I'm ready to take a break from writing, so I'm going to take them for a walk. But I will also use this opportunity to reinforce their "resting-quietly-while-mom-types" behavior by marking it (no clicker necessary for this already fluent behavior, so I'll just say, "Yes!") and then rewarding it (by standing up, putting on my sandals and grabbing their leashes).

The situation can be the "command"

You could interpret this by saying they aren't getting their beloved walk for free. After all, they earned it by choosing to rest while I worked. It's important to realize, though, that they were not responding to any commands from me. They were responding instead to the environmental cues around them: Mom touching the keyboard → take a nap. I didn't need to tell them what to do. This means I can retire from the job of "issuer of orders to dogs" and instead invest my attention and energy in improving my Seeing, Marking and Rewarding.

Of course, I do want the dogs I live and work with to know how to respond correctly to a variety of cues I give. These could be words I say to them (e.g., "Sit" or "Dance"), gestures I make (e.g., reaching toward Nick's front leg to ask him to place his paw in my hand) or tactile stimuli (e.g., tapping the tip of Nick's nose to ask him to sneeze). The SMART x 50 protocol accommodates these trainer-requested good behaviors. It is no violation for the trainer to cue the dog to do something that the trainer will See, Mark and Reward. But it also acknowledges a broader category of cues, beyond those produced by people. It recognizes that the external environment triggers behaviors in dogs, too; it also "issues commands" as does the internal, physiological environment of the dog. (Actually, it's a false distinction to say that the environment presents some cues to the dog and people present other cues to the dog. People are a component of, not separate from, the dog's environment.)

With SMART x 50, the source of the cue for the dog's good behavior is less critical than it is in NILIF. Both major sources of cueing—humans and the rest of the dog's environment—are valid and important. It may seem that removing the trainer from the role of commander-in-chief erodes the human's leadership. But isn't it more efficient to let the sounds, sights and other stimuli surrounding the dog directly signal good behaviors that the human can then skillfully See, Mark and Reward? Which would you prefer: a dog who moves to his bed and calmly lies there when you say "Park it" or a dog who does these behaviors as soon as the doorbell rings? This is a trick question—you want both. But it's pretty nifty when a dog responds to the doorbell by immediately running to his bed, or to the sight of his leash by sitting or to a person approaching to greet him by planting his front paws on the ground—all without verbal or gestural "Do this now" signals from a human.

Be a choice architect

One oft-neglected form of trainer input that hugely improves the efficiency of SMART is control of the dog's environment. "Set the dog up for success" is a cliché, but true nonetheless. I recently heard the term "choice architect" used by a behavioral economist to describe the people whose job it is to arrange products on grocery-store shelves to maximize the money consumers spend. While you shop, no one is standing beside you, commanding or physically manipulating you to pick a particular item. But your choice of products nonetheless is influenced strongly by the meticulously planned lay-out of that store.

In the same way, we want to influence the behavioral choices our dogs make. But when we use force to compel dogs to behave a certain way, we can't call that behavior voluntary: there is no choice. Allowing dogs to make choices without our coercion (e.g., pushing, pulling, leash-popping, grabbing, squirting, shocking) is therefore ideal; it removes us from the role of "making" the dog's behavior happen. Instead, the dog is responsible for making his own behavior happen. Our vital role is to notice more of those choices, inform the dog when he's chosen correctly and reward the dog so he'll be more likely to choose that way in the future.

Clever trainers stack the deck in their favor. They give the dog freedom to make choices, but they narrow the options. I'm reminded of my friend who each morning lays out two outfits on her young daughter's bed and then asks her whether she wants to wear the pink dress or the yellow one to kindergarten that day. The girl chooses, but between two acceptable options, rather than from the hundred pieces of clothing in her stuffed closet. Limitless choices are paralyzing, for dogs and for people.

Being a choice architect for your dog means that you'll make his "bad" behaviors (often the actions that come naturally to dogs) harder to do and his "good" behaviors (often the actions less hard-wired in the dog) easier. For example, you may place a thick fleecy dog-bed on the floor near the couch and also slant the couch cushions off horizontal. When your dog enters the room, looking for a place to rest, the dog-bed will likely be preferable to the off-kilter couch cushions. You, having set the stage, are prepared to See, Mark and Reward your dog's choice to curl up on the dog-bed rather than the couch. After you've rewarded your dog's voluntary but "situationally influenced" choice a couple dozen times, you can start gradually moving the couch cushions into a more normal—and tempting to the dog—position. You'll still See, Mark and Reward his correct choice of resting spot frequently while he's learning this discrimination, and intermittently once he has a well-established habit of choosing the dog-bed over the normally-positioned couch cushions.

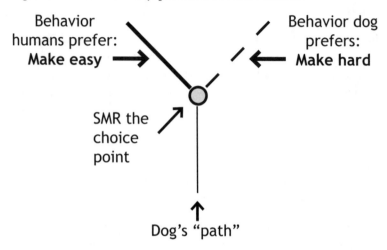

It's worth pointing out one other bit of environmental engineering my clients often resist. Large windows facing a busy sidewalk are an attractive nuisance for many dogs. It's here that they while away their days, repeatedly lunging and barking at passersby (i.e., strangers, dogs, bicycles, delivery personnel). Don't facilitate this hobby. Until your dog has learned an acceptable replacement behavior, it's best to block her view. Use blinds, thick paper, plywood, or as one of my clients did, aluminum foil. (Remember, it's temporary.) If your dog is using a piece of furniture as a perch to get a better look, move it away. Or keep her out of the room with the window by shutting the door or gating it off. Also, provide some other form of entertainment for your dog than practicing her "intruder alert and repel" trick.

Which behaviors to See, Mark and Reward

Before you can See, Mark and Reward your dog's good behaviors, you need some idea of what those behaviors look like. I ask clients to name three or four actions—not attitudes, not vagaries, not "dead-dog behaviors" (i.e., things a dead dog can "do" such as not barking or not pulling on leash)—they want to see their dog do more often. I say, "Imagine your dog is being good, however you and your family define this. What exactly is he doing?"

For dogs staying in my house for any length of time (my own newly-adopted dogs or clients' dogs whom I occasionally board), here is the short list of behaviors I try to See, Mark and Reward from the first day, in general order of priority:

1. pee and poop on grass (or other human-preferred substrate)

2. touch your nose to fingertips (mine or any person's)

3. glance at my face

4. move toward your dog-bed (or crate) and get "stuck" there (i.e., bed = large magnet sucking dog onto it)

5. move floorward (usually lie down, but alternatively could be sit or bow)

6. walk with me by my side

7. relax into current position (usually lying down) because you'll be there for a while

8. have "octopus paws" (i.e., pads of front paws suctioned to the ground) when any person approaches

9. back up a couple of steps

10. hold a toy in your mouth.

This is my list, for now. Priorities change. Your list of key behaviors will likely be different. That's fine. We all have our own picture of what a "good dog" actually does. Just keep in mind that though dogs are behaviorally flexible, they usually have trouble doing nothing for long stretches of time. They have to move. So make sure you're creating a "to do" list of behaviors, rather than a "don't do" list.

If you're new to training, I hope your list is shorter. Seeing, Marking and Rewarding just two or three behaviors is plenty to start with. Though the process takes conscious intention and attention for beginning trainers, it becomes intuitive after some consistent practice.

Like riding a bicycle or driving a car with a standard transmission, what initially seemed impossible to coordinate and execute becomes a completely fluent skill.

50 rewards a day! Really?

Once my client has identified a few behaviors she wants to see her dog do more often, we explore ways for her to See, Mark and Reward each one several times per day, with an overall goal to deliver fifty rewards to the dog each day. If there's only one human in the house, that person is responsible for doling out all fifty rewards. If there are more people, the job of rewarding can be split between family members, but this requires that everyone agree on which specific behaviors are reward-worthy.

When I first introduce SMART x 50 to my clients, I suggest that they use food as the reward for the dog. That means the dog will receive fifty bits of food from people in the household each day, as the consequence for doing various useful or cute behaviors. Of course, there are myriad other ways to reward dogs; we'll discuss these later in this chapter. But limiting the formula to "See, Mark and Feed" is usually simplest for beginning trainers.

Is it best to deliver these fifty food rewards in one concentration of largesse or in spurts throughout the day? Either is fine. Whatever works. Honestly, I'd prefer that my clients develop the ability to scan for their dog's good behavior all the time, whenever they're near the dog. However, it's often easiest for people to begin by choosing one or two times a day—maybe out on a walk or after the family has eaten dinner—when they can devote some of their over-burdened attention to the dog. Five very brief sessions of clicker-training, each lasting just one minute, would fulfill the quota as long as the rate of clicks and treats is at least ten per minute.

In this protocol, food is a vital training tool. Therefore, it's beneficial to consider which food treats work best for most dogs. Treats must fulfill several criteria; in general, they should be tiny, meat-based, soft, healthful, relatively inexpensive and convenient for the people doing the training. The arsenal of treats I use nearly every day, with my own dogs and with clients' dogs, includes: 1) inexpensive homemade turkey meatloaf (recipe is at www.kathysdao.com), 2) canned dog-food loaded into a plastic squeeze tube, 3) pureed meat baby-food (which the dog can lick directly from the jar), and 4) tiny kibble made from a unique protein source (e.g., rabbit, salmon).

Lickable food (2 and 3) is especially useful for small dogs for whom it is difficult to grab and hand out teeny bits of solid treats. For really small dogs, the treat may be one drop of slightly-diluted canned dog-food, dispensed with a 10-cc syringe.

I recently attended a full-day Tellington TTouch workshop with my dog, Effie. Another participant brought her gorgeous athletic Chihuahua and worked with this not-quite-four-pound dog all day. At the end of the workshop, as we were leaving, I asked the woman if she thought that recommending fifty food-rewards per day seemed absurd when your dog weighs less than a gallon of milk. She smiled, and then told me she routinely feeds that many treats per day; she enjoys training. I asked how she did this while still managing to keep her dog so beautifully lean. She leaned toward me, conspiratorially, and almost whispered, "I break the treats into really small pieces." I had to chuckle. No complicated solution, but instead a great trainer who has mastered the skill of grabbing and delivering to her small dog one itsy-bitsy treat at a time.

When possible, I do prefer using discrete pieces of food (e.g., bits of homemade meatloaf, tiny portions of commercially-produced meat-based treats) rather than having the dog lick out of a tube or a jar. This allows a family to easily keep track of each day's reinforcers. One family member can be responsible for preparing the dog's daily ration of treats ahead-of-time. At Sea Life Park oceanarium in Hawaii, where I conducted my thesis research, one staff person worked alone during the graveyard shift, thawing, sorting and weighing the tons of smelt, herring and mackerel that constituted the next day's meals for the many dolphins and whales. We called him the "fish phantom." So each family can have an assigned "treat phantom," responsible for cutting and counting fifty treats and then placing them in a plastic baggie, one baggie for each dog. This can be done every evening in preparation for the next day, or once a week in preparation for the next seven days. Starting each day with fifty treats in a container (in the fridge for treats that need it or on the kitchen counter) makes it easy to keep track. You know that by the end of the day, the container(s) should be empty. It also allows various family members to grab a few treats any time they want to do some training.

In any humane training protocol, the health and welfare of every animal is paramount. Obesity is a pervasive problem affecting the physical and behavioral health of dogs across the United States (and many other developed countries as well). Given this, the use of frequent food rewards must not cause any weight gain. This is accomplished by cutting back the amount of kibble (or alternate main food, such as a home-cooked or a raw diet) given to the dog at mealtimes. For some dogs, it may be appropriate to cut back to one meal a day instead of two, at least during the early stages of training, to allow the saved calories to be used as rewards. Or it may mean that kibble will comprise some of the daily treat quota. However you choose to accomplish it, SMART x 50 must not result in a fat dog. Ever.

This requires that the treats be nutritional meal replacements, not junk food. If you feed a raw or home-cooked diet (as I do), you can put some of this food in a squeeze tube and use it as "treats." For dogs with food allergies, you may have no choice but to use their prescription kibble—or the canned version in a food tube—as treats. Be especially careful not to feed too high a proportion of treats to small dogs; their digestive systems can be more sensitive to upset and to serious complications (e.g., pancreatitis). In all cases, consult with your veterinarian if you have any concerns that the treats you're using may pose any health risk to your dog.

For folks new to feeding tidbits to their dog so frequently, this will feel strange. It smacks of spoiling. Just this morning, while walking my dogs on the beautiful Tacoma waterfront, I passed a jogger named Terry. She always stops to pet my dogs; this has become something of a pre-dawn ritual for us all. Today, when she saw me hand Effie and Nick a couple of kibble, she remarked, "Oh, you're spoiling these dogs." I replied, "Actually, I'm feeding them breakfast."

Of course, I typically hand-feed these kibbles at precise times: for Effie, as she passes another dog with grace and composure, and for Nick, any time he's startled by a stranger's sudden movements near him. This process takes little effort on my part, other than remembering to carry a few treats whenever we're headed out of the house. (Just as I'd never leave home with my dogs sans clean-up bags, I never leave home without some food rewards. "Poop bags in one pocket, treats in the other.") It's an unfortunate truth that the delivery of food to a dog in any way other than a bowl at mealtime is, to many people, equivalent to spoiling.

Training junkies like me love data, so we tend to want to encourage our clients and students to keep track of which behaviors they've reinforced. Though I understand the benefits, I rarely ask beginners to record in any way beyond merely counting the fifty daily rewards they provide. I know that if they at least provide the frequent rewards, they'll start to see desired changes in the dog behaviors they've reinforced. The requirement to fill out detailed data sheets or behavior logbooks actually can discourage people from the inclination to "just do it" (i.e., reward the dog) whenever the urge strikes.

Some clients enjoy counting the number of daily "See, Mark and Rewards" they give their dog because it becomes sort of a game. This version of keeping score—where you count how many rewards you provide each day for good behavior—allows us to take advantage of our competitive nature. We can strive to top our own score. Competing with ourselves to become better rewarders is infinitely preferable to competing with the dog to determine who's boss.

It's easy to use variations of SMART x 50 to accommodate the needs of different family situations. As an example, for dog owners who've never used food treats as behavioral rewards, beginning with a goal of fifty per day is unrealistic. This is analogous to recommending "10,000 steps per day" to a completely sedentary person. A better plan would be to start with some fraction, say SMART x 10 (or, in the case of exercise, 2,000 steps per day) for one or two weeks. From there, the revised goals can be "more than before." An increase every week of five rewards per day would be one way to accomplish this.

I can think of situations in which this gradually increasing quota may still seem too daunting. For instance, a family with parents who work full-time, kids in school and three or more dogs at home is already time-starved. For them, it makes sense to adapt the SMART x 50 goal. Maybe they'll choose to follow SMART x 25 for each dog. Or they may decide on SMART x 50 as a daily goal for all their dogs combined. Whatever the accommodation, it's crucial that the objective remain ambitious (or "aspirational" as one colleague put it). It should be challenging enough to foster continuing behavioral development for the dogs, but not so discouraging that the humans give up trying.

Alternately, you can follow a more free-form version of SMART, with no daily quota. I once worked with a family with three Bullmastiffs. They wanted to improve the general manners of their huge dogs in preparation for a visit from a case-worker who'd be evaluating their home for the potential arrival of a foster child. A couple of weeks after our initial consultation, I contacted them to see how things were going. The wife reported that they'd adapted my recommendations to suit their busy schedules and multiple dogs. They put a big bowl of healthy treats in the center of their large kitchen island, where the dogs couldn't reach it. Any time any family member noticed any of the dogs being good (e.g., yielding space to a human, looking out the front window at passersby without barking), they grabbed a treat and tossed it to the dog. Once the container was empty for the day, there were no refills until the next day. I was concerned that the treats might be doled out unevenly, with one or two dogs getting "shorted." But I've observed that people tend to want to treat their dogs equally; they apply egalitarian rules when rewarding dogs (even when this is unnecessary or counter-productive). So all three of their dogs received a decent share of the bounty.

When can I stop?

Trainers who use food rewards often hear this question from their students: "When can I stop rewarding my dog with food?" Yet I'm betting veterinarians never hear from their clients, "When will I be able to stop feeding my dog every day? It's such a hassle and expense."

When we bring a new dog into our family, we take for granted that we'll feed that animal at least once or twice a day forever. Daily calories are obviously a non-negotiable need.

Given this, I have no problem using a small portion of my own dogs' daily rations to reward their good behaviors every day for the rest of their lives. It isn't a matter of feeding them more; it's rather just a redistribution of their food throughout the time I spend with them. They usually receive several food rewards during our morning walks, several more during afternoon play sessions in our yard and possibly a few more during evening training sessions in our living room.

I rarely See, Mark and Feed either of my dogs fifty times per day any more. Now that they're older (Effie is 13 years old and Nick is 10 years old), their behavioral repertoires are pretty stable. I currently am not teaching them new tricks or sports. So I'm likely to use a couple of dozen food rewards per dog per day to maintain the cute and useful behaviors they already know. Thanks to the incredible power of intermittent reinforcement, these sporadic food rewards suffice to sustain my dogs' retirement repertoires. Once you are satisfied with your own dog's repertoire—you aren't attempting to create, repair or replace any behaviors—you may decide to cut back to Seeing, Marking and Feeding x 20.

This doesn't mean you can't keep your daily SMART goal at fifty. You will just replace many of the treats you used as rewards during the initial training (i.e., the acquisition phase) with non-food rewards later in the training (i.e., during the maintenance phase). We'll discuss this alternative in more detail later in this chapter, but for now, be assured that the use of frequent food rewards can lay the foundation for a truly trusting relationship between you and your dog. It opens up the possibility that your dog will find your attention, touch, praise, play and presence increasingly rewarding. Also, as your dog's behavior improves, you'll be more apt to bring her into potentially rewarding situations (e.g., walks in the woods, play-dates with dog friends, etc.). The menu of "payment options" you can use to achieve fifty daily repetitions of See, Mark and Reward expands as a natural by-product of long-term use of first food, and then additional positive reinforcements.

Let's go back to the "10,000 steps per day" analogy mentioned earlier. When I first started trying to achieve this fitness goal for myself, I had to carve an hour out of my schedule to fit in a decent walk once a day. It was an effort. It was also separate from the rest of my life, something simply to cross off my "to do" list. Over the course of a couple of months, however, I began seeing the clear benefits of my obligatory walking (e.g., more stamina, better sleep, time for prayer), so I got hooked. Just as importantly, I was able to start integrating the basic concept—taking more steps whenever possible—throughout my typical daily routine (e.g., while talking on the phone with clients, by parking far from store entrances, etc.). Adding a few steps whenever I could became a habit, easily integrated into my life.

The same progression can be seen in people adopting SMART x 50 per day. At first, the goal may seem excessive and maybe impossible. It takes effort, planning and a dedicated chunk of time each day. Gradually, though, your new skill becomes second nature. Noticing your dog's good behavior, marking it and then rewarding it—initially with food most of the time and later with alternate reinforcers most of the time—meshes seamlessly with your other daily activities.

You might find that you can maintain your dog's good behavior with fewer than fifty repetitions of SMART each day, but this will depend on your dog's initial level of "behavioral fitness." Just as 5,000 steps per day may be enough to provide a fitness foundation for a lean teen, SMART x 25 may be enough for your easy-going, sociable Lassie. For your "dog with issues" or your canine competitor, SMART x 50 may remain your benchmark for as long as necessary.

Ignore harmless nuisance behaviors
Some "bad" behaviors are annoying but harmless. They're minor nuisances, best handled by ignoring them. I recently worked with a client, Mary, with a Cocker Spaniel puppy who liked to pick up things in her mouth in the yard. The pup wasn't swallowing or even chewing the pinecones or the worms or the leaves. She was just curious—picking them up, feeling them in her mouth. Mary was horrified: "These things have germs!" So, every time her dog mouthed a pinecone, Mary harassed and reprimanded her, with plenty of drama and volume, to drop the thing. I spent an hour explaining to Mary that it was okay to ignore this innocuous behavior because the puppy would likely stop doing it as soon as Mary stopped paying such intense attention to it.

Last year, I received a call from a prospective client and I had to keep asking if I really understood what he was saying. It's easy to get the wrong idea when you're conducting "problem triage" over the phone. The man kept repeating, "He's doing that bull thing." That bull thing? "Oh, wait," I asked. "Is this after he pees?" "Yes," the man replied, explaining that they'd just gotten new landscaping, so they needed their Jack Russell Terrier to stop that shuffling with his paws immediately. I asked how long the dog spent doing these paw-kicks. He replied, "A few seconds, several times a day." I asked what else the dog was doing that was a problem. "Nothing." Goodness. I wanted to suggest that this man relax a bit about the small imperfections in their pristine landscaping that a 15-pound dog can cause by 30 seconds per day of rubbing his paws along the grass. Instead, I suggested the man take his dog on walks for potty breaks or else provide a dedicated area in the yard for the dog's toileting needs.

Other less-than-perfect behaviors I choose to ignore in my own dogs include grabbing each other's toys, walking a pace ahead of me on leash, barking a few times at the mailman on the porch, digging shallow holes in my yard, lounging on the couch and chasing squirrels in the yard. Your choices will differ about which potentially pesky behaviors matter to you and which don't. Just consider that perfection is vastly overrated. You can safely let some things slide.

Prevent dangerous or destructive behaviors
An essential part of training any pet dog is to establish tendencies to inhibit or redirect the barking, peeing, jumping, grabbing, chewing and biting that are part of their genetic heritage. We can't simply ignore behavior that is destructive or dangerous (to people or to other animals or to the dog himself), hoping it will disappear.

To stop these untenable behaviors, mustn't we balance our several dozen daily "yeses" with an equal amount of "noes"? Well, no. Not if we take advantage of various ways we can physically limit the dog's activities while he is learning behaviors that will eventually counteract some of his canine instincts. Remember, our behaviorism motto says, "Prevent reinforcement for behaviors we don't want our dogs to repeat." Management tools can be used judiciously to limit the dog's opportunities to make undesired (by us) behavioral choices.

These temporary "choice limiters" include closed doors, baby gates, crates (wire, plastic, canvas), exercise pens (analogous to a toddler's playpen), tethers and basket muzzles.

Just last week, I consulted with a woman who had a litany of behavioral problems with her eight-month-old Pug mix. Among other things, it seems that Snuggles launches herself onto people's plates as they eat a meal. "She actually leaps up and puts her paws on our plates so she can grab food," said Mrs. G. When I asked how long this had been going on, she replied, "For months and months, even though we squirt her with a water bottle and keep yelling 'No!' Why won't she understand what 'no' means?" I pulled out of my gear bag a four foot long, coated-cable tether. I asked, "When you eat your meals, could you attach one end of a tether like this to Snuggles' harness and the other end to a table leg or an eye-bolt in the baseboard of your wall? You can put a comfy dog-bed nearby and you can even toss Snuggles a treat whenever she settles on the bed. You'll be rewarding her for a whole new way of begging: quietly lying on her bed, hoping for a tidbit. Eventually, you'll be able to stop using the tether because Snuggles will learn that resting on her bed makes you toss her a treat occasionally." The client thought she could do this. Then she began brainstorming other ways she could limit Snuggles' bad choices—by using a small playpen to keep her from jumping on visitors' laps, by papering over the lower half of the glass door to prevent her from barking at pedestrians on the nearby sidewalk. By looking at the situation from a new perspective—that of a choice architect—Mrs. G. finally was creating opportunities for her to be the source of treats for Snuggles' desired behaviors rather than the source of threats for Snuggles' bad behaviors.

Alternative 2: Create a photo album of your good dog

This probably should be labeled Alternative 1B. It's really a SMART x 50 extension that emphasizes the function of the marker signal. This marker could be an acoustic stimulus (a click, a "Yes," a whistle-toot), a tactile stimulus (one I sometimes use with dogs is a touch to the dog's occipital protuberance—the bony bump on the top of their head), or a visual stimulus (a "thumbs up" gesture, a flash from a penlight).

Marker signals provide essential information to the trainee. They pinpoint the exact behavior that "produces" reward. They serve as conditioned positive reinforcers and so strengthen the behaviors they coincide with. They indicate when a reward is available to the animal, and so their absence means that a reward is not available. (This is why using a marker signal with food-obsessed animals provides a big advantage. The absence of a click is information telling greedy dogs that they will not have access to treats until a click happens first, even though the trainer has food within reach.) Markers also elicit happy emotions in the trainee. And they help bridge delays between the animal's performance of the reward-worthy behavior and the trainer's delivery of the reward.

Understanding the functional significance of marker signals is crucial for professional trainers. However, when I'm selling a new student on why he should consider toting around a clicker for a while, I usually skip these technical details. Instead, I might ask him to pretend the clicker is a camera and to imagine that his thumb pressing the clicker button is actually pressing the shutter-button on a camera photographing his dog.

Karen Pryor, clicker-training pioneer and author of the timeless classic *Don't Shoot the Dog*, first taught me this analogy of "clicker as camera." It's simple and concrete. And because using a camera is so familiar, it makes people more comfortable trying this odd little gadget for the first time. Even though my new clients may never have seen clicker-training in action, they are likely fluent at taking photos with a point and shoot camera or their mobile phones.

I add another aspect to the analogy, asking students to use their clicker/camera to create a photo album of their good dog. "I want you to compile as many photos as you can of Max being good" (or "sweet" or "smart" or "calm" or "an angel"—depending on how I want to influence what behaviors they're looking for). I continue, "The click takes the photo and the treat pastes it into the album." I imagine this album as an actual three-dimensional book with paper pages and those tiny self-adhesive corners holding the printed photos in place. More tech-savvy folks probably envision a virtual photo album (think Flickr or Shutterfly). No matter; the analogy works either way.

Speaking of technology, it's likely this analogy will become obsolete as cameras continue getting smaller and cheaper. I can foresee the day when my clicker takes actual pictures and downloads these into a virtual photo album. Of course, you could use a small camera now as a marker signal. But using my IPhone's camera to take actual photos of my dog being good, and having the sound of the on-screen shutter be the dog's marker signal, seems incredibly unwieldy.

This camera analogy allows me to suggest another idea to my students. Only they know what Max's photo album should look like. They, along with other family members, get to choose which dog behaviors make them happy (or proud or relieved). I'm often surprised by the behaviors my clients want their dogs to perform (e.g., stand on their rear legs with their front paws on the person's shoulders, lick the dishes in the dishwasher, chase birds out of the yard). But this is pretty much irrelevant. It's their photo album.

Trainers know that the likelihood of a dog doing any particular behavior is dependent on that behavior's reinforcement history: the cumulative record of all the consequences (i.e., reinforcements and punishments) that have been associated with the behavior. Frequent, timely, generous, meaningful reinforcement of desired behaviors etches them into the dog's repertoire (unless countervailing punishers are given for the same behavior). So, continuing our analogy, we can say that the best albums contain thousands of photos.

Trainers also know that animals don't categorize their rewarded behaviors into "silly tricks" vs. "formal obedience moves." Any dog behavior that produces a consistent reward will go up in frequency, whether it's a snappy recall away from a squirrel or waving bye-bye. The album can hold photos of dozens of different behaviors. I tell clients, "If the behavior is useful or cute, click it." (And follow the click with a reward, of course.) This allows people to create a broad range of dog behaviors; at the same time, they are accumulating many rewards for a few key behaviors most important to them.

When I began teaching clicker-training to dog owners, I was humbled by one student who attended the first-week orientation class. As soon as he picked up a clicker for the first time, his click-timing was near perfect. Throughout the warm-up exercises of having the students click my right foot lifting off the ground, or click a tossed tennis ball as it hit the wall, Dane clicked at precisely the right instant. Turns out he was a professional photographer. He'd already been Seeing and Marking good "behavior"—in his photography subjects—for years. Too bad his dog was a young Bloodhound. Daisy was adorable, but she moved like cold molasses. Dane's amazing timing was not so necessary for a dog who took 10 seconds to lie down!

Alternative 3: Behavioral opportunities as rewards

Animal training is an application of the science of learning. Thank goodness, because this means we dog trainers can "cheat." Researchers studying the behaviors of rats and pigeons and monkeys in experimental settings may seem far removed from our practical training goals, but some techniques transfer readily from lab(oratory) to Lab(rador Retriever).

Reinforcement is the name of the game in animal training. By reinforcing a behavior, we make it stronger, that is, more likely to happen. So we invest great effort into reinforcing dog behaviors we like (e.g., lying quietly on a mat, running toward us, looking at us when we call the dog's name). We use food, our attention, toys, play and praise to reinforce these desired behaviors in our dogs.

There is another perspective on what reinforcement actually is: the Premack Principle. Defined in the 1960s by Dr. David Premack, professor emeritus of psychology at the University of Pennsylvania, this theory says that "high probability behavior reinforces low probability behavior." William O'Donohue and Kyle E. Ferguson (in *The Psychology of B.F. Skinner*) state it slightly differently: "Reinforcement is the opportunity to exchange a less valued activity for a more valued one." (p. 246)

Dr. Premack's pioneering insight is that an animal's behavior is reinforced whenever the consequence of that behavior is that the animal gets the opportunity to engage in an activity he would freely choose to do at that moment. For example, for a sociable dog, the opportunity to greet another dog (highly probable) would reinforce the behavior of lying down first (less probable). Keep in mind that many behaviors we'd like our dogs to do are relatively improbable (before training) because they're not part of the typical canine repertoire (e.g., keeping paws on the ground when greeting a human visitor, walking beside us). Our goal in training is to make them more likely. We use reinforcement to do this.

The Premack Principle asserts that reinforcement is not a thing (e.g., a piece of liver), but access to a preferred activity (e.g., eating tasty food). At any moment, if you can accurately predict which behavior your dog is most likely to do, you have identified a powerful reinforcer. The chance to chase a squirrel up a tree can reinforce heeling. Freedom to return to sniffing another animal's urine can reinforce coming away from a distraction when called. For a shy dog, darting to a hiding place under a chair can reinforce taking one step toward a stranger.

I once received an email from a talented young trainer asking if a particular dog-training scenario she described was an example of the Premack Principle. I answered that as far as I understood it, all reinforcement is an example of the Premack Principle. It is an all-encompassing theory, intended to provide a framework for every aspect of "reward" in training.

Every time you set up a situation in which your dog gains access to a highly likely activity, contingent on doing a behavior you like, you win. So does your dog. Those activities your dog loves—your dog's passions—might be considered distractions to training. But, when cleverly applied, they also can provide highly effective reinforcement, essential for creating strong, reliable behaviors.

One other thing about the Premack Principle: like gravity, it's in effect all the time, whether you understand it and capitalize on it or not. Whenever your dog "swaps" a less preferred activity for a more preferred one, reinforcement occurs and the future probability of the less likely behavior increases. Practically, this means that any time a "big thrill" occurs for the dog, the initiation of that event is a potent reinforcement opportunity. Big thrills are those enjoyable daily experiences that interrupt the monotony our dogs often experience: meals, walks, game-time, bones or food puzzles, couch privileges, etc. In her book, *The Culture Clash,* uber-pithy Jean Donaldson puts it this way (p. 102): "Empty dogs play Frisbee." In other words, the puppy peeing outside in the right place (lower probability behavior) results in an immediate round of a favorite game (higher probability). This increases the likelihood the puppy will pee on that substrate (and possibly in that location) in the future.

Notice that most pet dogs experience life as a series of relatively mundane stretches of time punctuated by Big Thrills. There may be breakfast (yum!) followed by humans getting ready for work (yawn) followed by a morning walk (yay!) followed by hours home alone (booorrring), followed by human arriving home (finally!), etc. You can capitalize on these moments of transition from dull to delight, turning them into reinforcement for behaviors you like, by using careful timing. Over the years, I've convinced my dogs that my on-switch for playing tug is them lying quietly on dog-beds. Tug is a Big Thrill for Effie and Nick, so I intentionally look for times when they are both resting angelically before I utter the coveted phrase, "Wanna tug?" Of course, doing this consistently for years has meant that the likelihood of them hanging out on their beds while I'm working at my desk is huge. I've so reinforced "settling," they would earn ribbons if there's ever a competition event for this.

Admittedly, the Premack Principle in its usual format—"high probability behavior reinforces low probability behavior"—isn't sticky. It's brief, but it isn't concrete or unexpected or narrative. It isn't even simple for anyone new to behavior modification.

One restatement of the Premack Principle that dog trainers commonly use is Grandma's Rule: "if you eat your broccoli, you can have dessert." Not bad, but this oversimplifies things. The Premack Principle is exciting and powerful because it embraces the always dynamic nature of reinforcement, acknowledging that with every occurrence of reinforcement of a low probability behavior, it becomes more probable. In fact, over a sustained history of reinforcement, that unlikely behavior may actually become more likely than the initial high-probability behavior; that is, the two behaviors can switch places on the probability hierarchy of the animal's behaviors. That means Grandma's Rule would have to account for the fact that sometimes a kid could be reinforced for eating dessert by getting an opportunity to eat broccoli. Not likely.

I'd like to offer an alternative metaphor that may serve as a trainer-friendly way to convey the essence of the Premack Principle. Groundbreaking horse-trainer and philosopher Alexandra Kurland (www.theclickercenter.com) wrote something several years ago as part of a lovely essay answering my question: "What is clicker training?" I'd asked this of a dozen of my training heroes because I wanted to extract the core principles on which they agreed. All the responses were illustrative and thoughtful, but only Alex's gave me chills. She managed to succinctly express the profound level of communication and cooperation inherent in this style of training. I think she also summarized what trainers need to know about the Premack Principle. Alex wrote:

> There are two sides to the click: what happens before and what happens after. What happens immediately before the click is a behavior the trainer would like to strengthen. What happens immediately after is an event the animal would like to strengthen, such as receiving food. The click unites these two desires.

When I first read this eloquent passage, I immediately pictured the click as the center fulcrum on a teeter-totter. For the animal, it is the "instant of exchange," when he can stop doing a lower probability behavior (e.g., moving away from a squirrel) and start doing a higher probability behavior (e.g., playing a round of tug, eating a meatball, or even running back toward the squirrel). With the click, the trainer says, "You've done enough good behavior for the moment;

now it's my turn to do some good behavior" (e.g., playing or feeding or releasing you). Note that the good behaviors our dogs are doing to make us click are typically lower probability stuff such as being "polite," demonstrating impulse control, or moving in precise non-doggy ways (e.g., weaving through a set of upright poles). Our click informs the dog that, yes, we will pay for that relatively unlikely behavior by providing him with a chance to do a more valued behavior.

Alex's definition of clicker training also conveys the two-way nature of the process and the deep and resonating joy that clicker trainers experience. We sometimes joke that this process is addicting, for both trainers and animals, but this is not far from the truth. This reciprocal exchange of reinforcement between learner and teacher—the animal behaving in a way that pleases the trainer, followed by the trainer behaving in a way that pleases the animal, over and over—is the very definition of a cooperative partnership. The rewards flow in both directions, with each partner taking turns behaving in desirable ways. Just like playing on a seesaw, the partners alternate being on top and being on the bottom, not in the sense of dominance or sub-ordinance, but in terms of being either the giver or the receiver of reinforcement.

Alternative 4: STILAFSA = some things in life are free, some aren't

I'm surprised how often trainers (or other pet professionals such as veterinarians, veterinary technicians or shelter workers) recommend a NILIF program without also emphasizing the importance of first fulfilling the dog's basic physical and psychological needs. Do the dogs have a safe environment, shelter and protection from temperature extremes, water and nutritious food, some companionship, exercise and quiet time, and occasional changes of scenery? By not directly addressing these "minimum daily requirements" that sustain each dog's physical and mental health, we run the risk of implying that we can, ethics intact, begin a behavior-modification program by rationing everything and anything the dog finds valuable.

Here's a riddle: When is food not a positive reinforcer? One of several correct answers: When the animal is deliberately starved. To quote Dr. Murray Sidman's extraordinary book, *Coercion and Its Fallout:*

> *Another misuse of positive reinforcement is deliberately to create the kinds of deprivations that make reinforcers effective: Prisoners, first placed in solitary confinement, are then permitted social contacts as reinforcement for docility; first starved, they can then get food in return for subservience. Freedom and food look like positive reinforcers, but when they are made contingent on the cessation of periods of deprivation that others have imposed artificially, their effectiveness is a product of negative reinforcement; they become instruments of coercion. (pp. 46-47)*

This passage haunts me. It's eerily descriptive of the approach of some trainers who employ such radical rationing of freedom and food that the dogs are starving, physically and emotionally. In this case, provision of these "treats" does more than just satisfy the dog's desire; it actually provides relief from significant discomfort or even pain. This effect shifts them into the category of negative reinforcers, which, according to Dr. Sidman, have deleterious side effects on the animal's future behavior and mental health.

There's no escaping the challenge this insight presents to all trainers. Does it mean we should provide food, freedom and all other goodies ad libitum? Surely not. Just imagining giving our pet dogs free access to everything they want evokes a Lord-of-the-Flies scenario—chaotic, crazy-making and dangerous.

If we deem unacceptable each end of the continuum—both complete rationing of reinforcers and complete access to them—we need to decide where between them we'll draw the line. I advise clients that their dogs require some amount of food, freedom and fun every day, whether they "deserve" it or not. The specific amounts vary by situation, but completely withholding the dog's basic necessities in order to motivate compliance to some behavioral demand is unconscionable.

I understand the pull to do this, especially in cases in which a training goal is critical and the time available to accomplish the assignment is limited. When I trained dolphins to search for sunken mines and to attach explosives to the cables on those mines (for subsequent remote detonation), these tasks were quite challenging for the dolphins, both cognitively and physically. And we always had a deadline for completing this training thoroughly enough so that the dolphins could pass a stringent field test. The countdown clock was always ticking for us trainers.

It was tempting for us to consider withholding a dolphin's food for a day (or two) if he refused to participate in a training session. We could have rationalized the decision, saying, "No beaching, no food." But this would have been idiocy. Dolphins are mammals; they need fresh water every day and they obtain this from their food fish. Also, enduring a day or more without a meal simply makes dolphins sick and irritable, not "motivated."

And so, no matter how poorly a dolphin may have done during a day's training session, he was given minimum rations. Of course, we timed this meal so it did not reinforce the balking (i.e., we fed him hours after he opted out of a training session). Often, before we fed him, we tried to get at least a semblance of a cooperative response on an easier task. But even if he refused to perform any "good" behavior, he ate something every day.

Be aware that depriving animals of their minimal physiological and social needs can make them desperate. This can then manifest as pushy, demanding behavior (often misattributed to dominance) or as anxious, disengaged behavior (often misattributed to stubbornness).

For our dogs, some things in life are free (STILAF), or should be. That is, they are provided daily regardless of the dog's compliance with our training plans or behavioral expectations. Included in this category are fresh water, fresh air, minimum caloric requirements, shelter, safety from pain and fear, some freedom to move and stretch, some access to at least one companion and the unconditional positive regard of the caretaker(s)/owner(s).

This does not mean we must never use these things as reinforcers for the dog's desirable behaviors. For example, I can arrange a training trial so that when I arrive home from work, Effie grabs a toy, on cue, instead of jumping on me. Her toy-fetching behavior earns her the privilege of getting access to me (yes, for her this is a privilege). But I would not sequester her from me for a day (or even an hour) if she didn't merit the access. Dogs need to spend time with their family.

Another example: I will feed dogs their minimal calories every day (with a rare exceptions such as an occasional planned fast, or the brief period of one to two days sometimes needed to transition a finicky free-fed dog to one who robustly eats meals). Yet I still can use most or all of these calories to reinforce good behavior. I can try to make delivery of the food contingent on the dog doing something useful or cute. But—here's the catch—if the dog doesn't perform any behaviors I like, I'll still feed him. Before I hand over the food, I'll wait for the dog to do something as inoffensive as possible; we could call this the dog's least awful behavior (LAB for short). So, regardless of whether the dog is responsive to my cues, ignoring my cues or outright hostile to me—in all cases, a minimum amount of food is "free."

Do avoid the trap of providing any of these minimum daily requirements for your dog "on demand." (After all, you're not HBO.) Time their onset so your dog is doing something other than shouting with his behavior, "Give me that!" Obnoxiousness of any kind should be futile for your dog.

Given this, it would not be a contradiction to say that trainers/owners can designate some foods—and other reinforcers—as "earned only." That is, a few things in life are never free. These are events so special and thrilling for the dog that it would be a shame to waste their potential as behavior builders. They are the heavy-hitters on the reinforcement line-up; we want to capitalize on their power to shift behavioral repertoires.

My 13-year-old dog Effie has always reacted in the same way every time she sees a Kong retrieving dummy. She grabs the rope in her mouth and explodes in a paroxysm of bliss, running joy-laps, swinging the Kong back and forth as she bucks and bounds. Consequently, I reserve this toy as a training reward. It doesn't live in the toy-box on the living-room floor. I keep it on the top of my refrigerator, along with a couple of extra-special tug toys. I devise scenarios in which I can present my dogs with these too-good-to-give-away-for-free toys after I've marked (usually with a "yes" at this point in their training) some great behavior (e.g., resting on their dog beds while I type on my laptop or coming when I call them away from my neighbor at the fence).

One more example: inexpensive fast-food hamburgers make excellent reinforcers. Trainers can stash a hamburger in a remote location before bringing the dog into the area. I used to hide one or two in the branches of a tree along a wooded trail I'd later hike with my off-leash dogs. This gave me the opportunity to cue a recall ("Here!"), and after I'd marked their success with "Yes," we'd race together to the meat-bearing tree. I'd stand on tiptoes, stretching to grab the hidden hamburgers and then toss one to each dog. The surprise of receiving such an astounding prize often paralyzes dogs the first time it happens, but they quickly figure out how to gleefully wolf down their reward.

I can't imagine a situation where I'd hand over a hamburger to either of my dogs "just because" (e.g., just because they're cute, just because I'm a loving caretaker, just because they want it). It's one reinforcer too valuable to waste.

This is, however, a slippery slope. Once you reserve a few good things to be always contingent on the dog's correct response to a cue (from the trainer or from the external environment), it's easy to throw more and more good things into this category. Then you quickly arrive right back at NILIF. So pick three things to ration completely. Or four maybe. Not ten. And not everything. Don't tumble to the bottom of this slope.

Alternative 5: Limited NILIF

You may decide to keep using and recommending NILIF, but with some restrictions. Here are a few options:

NILIF-For Now: It's possible to follow the NILIF protocol only for a set time, or until the dog reaches some specific behavioral or developmental milestone. One clear, well-explained example of this approach is detailed in the book, *Ruff Love* by Susan Garrett. She lays out a challenging multi-stage program whereby the dog gradually earns more freedom and privileges. Another plus: her recommendations are grounded in the language and tenets of behaviorism rather than emphasizing the need to teach dogs their place in the family hierarchy.

NILIF-For Kids: You might decide that strict reward-rationing is more important for some family members to do than others. Maybe in your house, Nothing In Life Is Free from the youngest children. This means you'll have different rules for various family members. Dogs can adjust to this, but it certainly complicates life when training and treat-dispensing routines vary among people living in the same house.

NILIF-For Starters: On rare occasions after meeting new clients, I will still choose to give them a NILIF protocol because I think it may be the best framework for behavioral advice, given their unique background and perspective. This may include dog owners currently using physically aversive techniques. Wanting to guide them through a transition from alpha rolls, leash pops and physical coercion, I may choose NILIF as an attainable first step along this path. It can serve as a non-threatening foundation—in the minds of both the dog and the people—bridging the way toward a less restrictive approach in the future.

I frequently work with pet owners who are (or have been) military personnel. NILIF may sometimes work well for folks with a history of military training. The rigorous rationing of privileges and the clear, one-way chain of command are familiar concepts. So, on occasion, I may decide to explain the basic training approach this way. I'm confident there are better approaches than NILIF for almost all of my clients, but I'll adapt and integrate it if necessary.

CHAPTER 6

Putting the Heart Before the Force: Dog Training as Spiritual Practice

After a decade conducting behavior consultations with hundreds of dog owners, a few cases still haunt me. It's been several years since I arrived at the elegant suburban home of a new client, Mrs. H., at the appointed time. She'd called me the previous week, worried that the family's new dog was a danger to her two young daughters. Sassy had snapped at the girls when they approached her during mealtime. "We can't have that in our home," said Mrs. H.

I soon discovered that Sassy, a glossy black Spaniel mix, was the family's first dog and that she'd been adopted from a local animal shelter a few months earlier. She greeted me in the foyer with bouncy, goofy exuberance, until Mrs. H. reprimanded her and pulled her away. We all moved into the living room where I met the two young daughters. As sometimes happens, the girls commenced trying to monopolize my attention. So I started looking at and speaking to them only when they weren't screaming or poking the dog.

I also conducted a standard interview with Mrs. H., asking about Sassy's daily routine and behavioral history. I learned that Sassy spent many hours home alone most days, in a small yard, confined by an electronic containment system. I mentioned the dangers of this arrangement (e.g., other animals and people have unfettered access to your yard and dog, confined dogs may at times cross the boundary to chase wildlife but then won't re-enter the yard, etc.) and the possible side effects of using shock as a training tool. Mrs. H. clearly wanted me to get to the point—to help her stop Sassy from being dominant to her kids.

While we chatted, I had an opportunity to observe her daughters' behavior toward Sassy. Tucked into a nearby nook under a small countertop sat a kibble-filled bowl. Intermittently, Sassy would approach that bowl to grab a mouthful. During a couple of these approaches, one or both girls popped out from behind the wall to surprise Sassy with a burst of petting and shrill giggling. It was evident to me that Sassy was wary about getting anywhere near that corner or her food. I'm sure she came to perceive that area as dangerous and the girls as a threat. Sassy's snapping was her way of telling the girls to give her some space. We likely could fix this misbehavior rather easily by changing Sassy's meal location and by giving her some privacy from pounces by small humans. We also could do some classical counter-conditioning training to create in Sassy better associations to the girls' approaches.

With this reasonably simple behavior-modification plan in my head, all ready to share with Mrs. H., I felt confident. But my good spirits were fleeting. I soon discovered a more insidious problem, one I could not repair.

I wanted to demonstrate how food rewards could help create enthusiastic, reliable behavioral responses in Sassy. Crouching with my back against one of the couches, I brightly called out "Sassy, here!" From across the room, the pup turned and dashed toward me. When she'd gotten just within arm's reach, she yelped so loudly that my heart froze. Sassy recoiled and whimpered. Startled and confused, I turned to Mrs. H. and told her I hadn't even touched Sassy.

I swear Mrs. H. smirked as she walked to the couch and pulled a plastic disk from underneath. "Oh, it wasn't you; it was this—we use it to keep Sassy off our couch." At the beginning of our session, I'd noticed on Sassy's collar the pronged radio-receiver typical of electronic containment systems used as outside "fences." What I hadn't known was that there were transmitters inside the home, too. When Sassy crossed the invisible boundary, getting "too close" to the couch, the receiver on her collar emitted a shock. And so, for enthusiastically racing toward me when I called her, Sassy felt a jolt of electricity. I was speechless—and nauseated. Then, to complete the nightmare, I noticed the girls laughing. Whether they were laughing at Sassy's misery or at my bewilderment, I couldn't know. But in that instant I did know that those girls would grow up to be Not Well. To witness on a regular basis such effortless casual cruelty to a living creature, a member of their family—to become so inured to force and coercion at such a young age—surely this must corrode the soul.

Quaking with emotion, I hurriedly ended our consultation and fled from this client and her home. I backed out their driveway, then parked down the block and sobbed. For weeks, I was troubled and preoccupied by the insanity of this case. I briefly considered stealing Sassy from their unfenced yard to rescue her from that psychologically poisonous house.

How is it that educated, well-intentioned people can decide it's morally acceptable to bring into their family a pet who will endure the torture of painful shocks, delivered both in the yard and in the house, to learn behaviors that easily could be taught through positive reinforcement or accomplished by a physical barrier? A pet who will be subjected to the frequent taunts of children who provoke her during meals? A pet who learns that the world is indeed threatening and full of things to fear?

Earlier this week, I had a conversation that echoed this low point in my work as a behavior consultant. During a morning stroll with my dogs along the waterfront, a stranger approached me to chat. She'd frequently seen us walking there, she said, and noticed that I had one more dog than usual. When I explained that Bridget was a client's terrier whom I was boarding for a few days, she realized I was a "pet professional." As any dog trainer knows, this is the cue for almost anyone to launch into a story about his or her own training challenges. And so the woman, who introduced herself as Sue, told me she occasionally has to walk her adult son's large dog. The problem is the dog pulls on the leash with gusto and lunges aggressively at passing dogs.

I asked what sort of collar or harness the dog was wearing, hoping to provide quick advice about head-halters or front-attachment harnesses. Sure enough, the dog wore a flat nylon collar attached to a retractable leash (i.e., a truly unworkable arrangement for any dog over 15 pounds). Then Sue mentioned that the dog also wore "the other collar"—a shock collar. Sue had been "zapping" the dog whenever he lunged, but it wasn't resolving the problem.

At that moment, our spontaneous pleasant conversation during my daily dog-walk/prayer-time began making my heart ache. I wanted to stop doling out free advice and walk off in the opposite direction to enjoy the sunrise in peace. Instead, I suggested that shocking her dog for being upset at the sight of an approaching dog was quite unlikely to teach him to be relaxed during future encounters. Sue explained that she often used just the warning tone and not the actual shock. Willing myself to breathe deeply, I replied that threats of causing pain aren't a whole lot more effective or humane than actually causing pain. Wielding a weapon is still coercive and frightening, even if you don't pull the trigger. (In these situations, I always imagine the absurdity of an armed robber trying to defend himself by saying, "But officer, all I did was hold a gun to the guy's head; I never fired!")

So far, this conversation was commonplace. Sadly, many folks think it's legitimate to use invasive invisible punishers such as shock collars to make dogs stop doing normal doggie behaviors for which it is relatively simple to teach acceptable replacement behaviors. What took our discussion to the level of insomnia-inducing for me was Sue's next off-hand comment—that she's been an elementary school teacher for twenty years. So I asked, "Do your students ever make mistakes, say in math class, or do they ever speak rudely to each other?" She wrinkled her mouth in the universal human expression meaning "duh!" and said "Of course." "And do you taser them when they do?" I asked. She said nothing. She was not amused. I pressed on, though, and said that animals suffer the same fear and pain when experiencing shock that humans do, only they can't give voice to their distress. The shock collar was deepening rather than resolving her problem. "Better tools and techniques exist," I told her, "and I can teach you about them." I smiled when Sue then asked for my business card. I hope to have the chance to help Sue experience the relief and the fun of switching from being a punisher to being a reinforcer—from being a source of threats to being a source of treats. Her son's dog will benefit, for sure, but more importantly, so will the hundreds of children whose lives she touches. And, just as significantly, so will Sue.

This last point is often overlooked in discussions about what constitutes humane dog training. It's a profession that includes a horrific history of outright abuse and violence and there's certainly plenty of work—educational, cultural and legal—we still need to accomplish to root out and replace methods that cause dogs pain and fear.

But what about the corrosive effect that pervasive punishment of dogs has on the punishers, on the hearts of the people doing the shocking, squirting, smacking or scolding? And, more subtly, might the frequent use of even passive-aggressive techniques with our dogs—shunning, withdrawing, being physically or emotionally unreachable, ignoring bids for attention—also sap the deep joy people experience when in collaborative communication with another species?

In my years as a dolphin and whale trainer, it was common for the zoo or the university research lab where I worked to receive requests from critically ill people, or the parents of very sick children. They'd want the opportunity to interact with the animals—to "commune" with them to achieve some relief from their symptoms. They believed the cetaceans had special healing powers.

At the time, I scoffed at this notion. Now I believe the petitioners were correct. Partly. Connecting with dolphins or whales—by touching them, talking to them, feeding them and cueing them to do behaviors—was, in fact, therapeutic. Invariably, the patients' spirits were lifted; they felt better. But the healing effect wasn't a gift uniquely attributable to these species. The key factor, I believe, was that the interactions between the patients and the cetaceans were voluntary. The animals always had a choice about how much they would participate.

I'd argue that the exact same life-giving effects those patients gained from their time with the dolphins is available to us all whenever we interact spontaneously and reciprocally with our dogs (or cats, or horses or birds, etc.). And aren't most people ill in some way—depressed, soul-weary, emotionally exhausted—and in need of this very sort of restoration? What an incredible benefit accrues to us when we choose non-coercive, behavior-generating methods of training. In fact, selfishness alone should drive people toward this philosophy of training. The dividend of joy that surges in us as we participate in such two-way communication with another creature is beyond measure.

Yet, "compulsion-based" vs. "positive reinforcement-based" polemics still play out on TV, in books and on blogs. For people outside the narrow world of professional dog trainers, the long-running debates about how best to train dogs may seem ridiculous. After all, they're only dogs, right?

Well, they are dogs, but there's no "only" about it. Besides being fully deserving of dignity in their own right, dogs can help us figure out how to get along with other beings, human and non-human. Living with dogs presents us with the paint-by-numbers version of relationships, helpfully simplified because it's stripped of the human complications of verbal language, spiteful (or altruistic) agendas, endless analysis and moral equivocating. Given dogs' sociability, matchless sensitivity to human body-language, behavioral flexibility and passion for physical play, they are ideal "lab partners" for humans desiring to develop new skills to become better parents, spouses, siblings and friends. This is why discussions about various dog-training methods can get so emotional. They reflect our deepest beliefs about how all relationships should function.

Obviously, I'm in the "treats rather than threats" camp in these discussions. In fact, I recently had the privilege of once again teaching at ClickerExpo, my eighteenth time working with an array of amazing instructors, each deeply committed to the principles of positive reinforcement. But there's a more subtle dichotomy in training approaches than this crucial distinction of "reinforce" vs. "force" —and it's as relevant to our relationships with people as it is to our relationships with pets.

Leader vs. feeder (or the big cheese vs. the big cheese dispenser)

The pioneering positive trainer Patty Ruzzo uttered the best line I've ever heard at a seminar. Twenty years ago, this brilliant instructor and champion dog-sport competitor said, "I don't know if my dogs consider me their leader and I don't care. They're greedy and I have their stuff." Pithy, and an elegant summary of the most fundamental law of behavior: postcedents (i.e., consequences), not antecedents, drive behavior. The reinforcements (and punishments) you provide your dog influence his future behavior far more than leaderly input such as assertive commands and physical prompting. In fact, the incredible power of operant conditioning comes from pulling behavior out of the behaver—through use of frequent, precise, intentional, meaningful reinforcement, in the case of clicker training—not by pushing the behaver to behave, literally or psychologically.

The term "leader" is surely vague enough to allow multiple interpretations. In dog training, however, it's often used to mean that humans go first (out doorways, when walking together down the sidewalk, eating meals, etc.) or are literally "on top" (sitting or sleeping higher, pinning the dog to the ground as a punishment, etc.). Being a leader also can mean that humans initiate all interactions with dogs, serving primarily as behavioral directors and commanders-in-chief. "Being alpha" is supposedly as much about having the correct (i.e., assertive and uncompromising) attitude as it is about the things you do.

We could view leadership differently, though. I'm reminded of a favorite quote by Nelson Mandela in his autobiography, *Long Walk to Freedom:* "A leader is like a shepherd. He stays behind the flock, letting the most nimble go out ahead, whereupon the others follow, not realizing that all along they are being directed from behind." (p. 22)

Could the best sort of leadership come "from behind?" Maybe it's actually less about commanding and controlling the learner—routinely telling him what to do—and more about setting up for, seeing, marking and rewarding the learner's freely offered cooperative behaviors. In this view, good leaders spend their energy thoughtfully arranging the learner's environment to promote good behavior, proactively planning to avoid problems and steering clear of interventions that create fear or avoidance. This quieter, more nuanced version of leadership seems somehow un-American. We're such a "get busy and make stuff happen" culture; it's challenging to stop, look and listen to our dogs.

At the risk of being branded a member of the "wussy collection" (a term that a Swiss colleague recently shared with me), I've come to believe that a dog trainer's main task is to be a skillful feeder, in the broadest sense of this word. Effective trainers are reward junkies (as, ideally, are the animals they train). They strive to be the source of dozens of things the dog finds satisfying: food, play, attention, affection, exercise, smells, praise, petting, freedom, comfort and more. They recognize and respect the power of these "satisfiers" to etch into the dog's repertoire particular behaviors. In this way, expert trainers try to ensure the dog's "good stuff" is contingent on acceptable behaviors, in other words, that the various reinforcers fuel dog behaviors that humans like. Equally important, they try to ensure that the dog's less-than-ideal (e.g., dangerous, destructive, demanding) behaviors do not "work" (i.e., they don't result in access to a reinforcer).

How is this different from NILIF? Aren't proficient trainers, in their role as feeder (i.e., the source of all variety of positive reinforcers), using the dog's "good things in life" in a calculated way? Yes, certainly. Training always involves some manipulation of environmental variables. There are at least two key differences, however: 1) some good things in the dog's life should always be free—love, air, water, safety, freedom from pain, terror or temperature extremes; and 2) even the remainder of the good things—especially food, play and attention—should not always be contingent on the dog's correct response to a command (or cue) from a human. They can be given to the dog any time he's acting "okay"—not perfect, submissive, obedient or deferent, but simply not threatening, obnoxious or balking (i.e., refusing a request to move).

Here's one more perspective on the "leader vs. feeder" question. My spirituality, informed mainly by Roman Catholicism (but with considerable cross-pollination by Buddhism and the book *A Course in Miracles*), emphasizes our human mission as being bread for the world. Jesus repeatedly urged His followers to feed the hungry and give sustenance to the poor. For Catholics, during Eucharist, bread and wine are transformed miraculously (the technical term is transubstantiated) into the Body and Blood of Christ, given for the life of His people. I am devoted to a God humble enough to share our humanity and loving enough to give Godself as food for us all. Feeding others, metaphorically and literally, is pretty much the job description for Christians.

If you were to attend Mass at my parish, St. Leo Church in Tacoma, Washington, you'd see something different than what occurs during most Catholic liturgies. At St. Leo, during Holy Eucharist, the priest distributes the sacred Bread to everyone in the congregation first, waiting until each person has eaten before receiving the Bread himself. This is deeply symbolic and so lovely that I find it distressing in other churches to witness communion done the standard way, where the priest eats and drinks first. At St. Leo, our priest fulfills his role as leader by feeding others first. Feeding (i.e., serving the needs of) the congregation is paramount. This manifestation of leadership in which "the last shall be first, and the first last" (Matthew 20:16) is topsy-turvy compared to the sort of "alpha goes first" leadership espoused by legions of dog trainers. Yet it is the very act of satisfying the needs of another—in trainer-speak, providing reinforcers—that creates real and long-lasting behavior change (i.e., transformation).

This upside-down quality of power, manifested so authentically at St. Leo Church, was never more moving to me than when Fr. Pat washed my feet. The main event of every Holy Thursday liturgy is a reenactment of Jesus' washing the feet of his disciples at the Last Supper. So, supplied with pitchers of warm water, basins and towels, we take turns having our feet washed by a fellow parishioner and then kneeling to wash the feet of the next person to approach and sit before us. In this simple physical ritual, we embody our mission to be self-effacing servants to one another.

It was twenty years ago, when I formally recommitted to being an active member of the Catholic Church, that I was assigned to be the first person to sit in front of the congregation to have my feet washed—by our pastor, Fr. Pat. Over the previous year, this fiercely brilliant and soulful man somehow had managed, through his inspired preaching and empathetic counseling, to open my heart to grace and to a God who loved me without condition. He was my respected teacher and spiritual leader, and yet he humbled himself to kneel before hundreds of people to pour water from a cobalt blue ceramic pitcher over my size 9½ feet. No words were necessary. The ritual itself conveyed to me, viscerally, all I needed to know about authentic leadership. It comes from setting aside our presumed status to pour ourselves out in service to one another.

Of course, this spiritual understanding of leadership bears no resemblance to the secular Western version that bombards us. In fact, if we were to draw a Venn diagram of these concepts, the two circles wouldn't even overlap. To reverse the status-seeking that practically defines our American culture is subversive. Yet, this idea that a true leader is one who readily serves the needs of (i.e., feeds) others provides me with a refreshing perspective on the hackneyed advice that a dog owner should be "leader of the pack."

Each morning that I wake to see my two old dogs eager to begin another day's adventures, I say aloud, "Thank you God for one more day with my companions." And I'm reminded that this word, so descriptive of their role in my life, translates literally to "bread fellows." (Turns out my dogs are my bed-fellows and my bread-fellows.) Companions are those you share food with, and this sharing of food, along with other satisfiers (i.e., reinforcers), in a generous and thoughtful way—this feeding—builds an enduring bond of trust and a pervasive spirit of cooperation.

Think of all the companions in your life: your friends, spouse, parents, children, siblings, employees, boss, neighbors, etc. Might you have the strongest effect on their behavior by seeking ways to fulfill their needs rather than by ordering, criticizing, snubbing, stonewalling or threatening them? Just imagine a world where the social norm for all forms of behavior modification was to maximize positive reinforcement while minimizing coercion. Would we have any idea how to handle the flood of satisfaction that would replace our habitual anxiety and avoidance? Might we discover that joy is everyone's birthright and that it's vastly more fulfilling than settling for mere temporary relief from the unrelenting pressures of modern life?

I vs. eye

Reflecting on the questionable usefulness of NILIF as the foundation and framework for sound dog-training advice, I kept bumping into another contrast. In its insistence that dogs get access to good stuff only as a result of deferring to a human's command (or cue), NILIF gives all the power to the people. Owners decide what dogs can do and when they can do it while discouraging dog-initiated reward-seeking behaviors. The emphasis is on what **I**, the trainer, need you, the dog, to do in order to earn any and all privileges. It could be called "iTraining" (perfect for a society rife with iPhones and iPads).

We now come to a topic on which I am, admittedly, an expert: ego. Surely this results, at least in part, from years of answering the idle question, "So what do you do for a living?" with the smug, "I train dolphins/whales/walruses for the University/Navy/zoo." I'm not sure how I even managed to haul around such an oversized "I" for so many years.

When I switched to training dogs, it was easy to follow a training regimen in which I, the trainer, required you, the animal, to obey me or else I'd withhold the things you need. It permitted me to follow the rules of good training while keeping my hubris intact.

But, as I've questioned both this approach and my relentless self-absorption, my training focus has shifted gradually away from ensuring animals' compliance with my directives. Instead, I've become increasingly aware of the critical need for me to observe the animals I train—intentionally watching their behaviors with mindful attention. This cultivation of the skills of clearly seeing behavior and learning to recognize and respond to desirable behaviors trumps any reward-rationing protocol. It also precedes—temporally and philosophically—any attempts I make to improve the animal's obedience to my requests.

My training has changed, replacing an "eye" for an "I." Dedicating energy to seeing "the other"—fully perceiving the range and subtlety of the animal's behaviors—has become the most important component of the training I do and the training I teach to my students.

A few months ago, I noticed myself saying to my dog, Nick, in a playful way, "I saw that!" I'd caught a glimpse of him air-scenting in the direction of an unfamiliar man standing near us in the park. I liked this subtle behavior of Nick's; it indicated curiosity and confidence. So I said, "Yes," praised him and tossed a treat. The thing is, I've also said "I saw that" to Nick and to other animals in a completely different tone of voice, where the phrase was intended as a reprimand (e.g., when I'd caught a dog starting to lift a leg to urine-mark the couch). It's much more fun to use that phrase in a game of catching animals correctly doing something—even a tiny something.

More so, in life beyond training, I've discovered that by quieting the "I scream" and releasing, even slightly, my death-grip on self-importance and pride, I begin to see more clearly. By emptying ourselves of ourselves, we all can make room for "the other" to enter our awareness. This is the heart of effective training—and of successful relationships.

Hierarchy vs. anarchy?

What happens if we trainers go even further, moving beyond making cognitive and emotional space for "the other"—in this case, the dog—to enter fully into the training process? Could we decide that training is, ideally, a partnership of sentient animals—one human and the other non-human—which has the goal of increasing the joy of both partners as well as everyone around them? Could training be a process which animates and gives life to our dogs instead of a process full of "corrections," behavior suppression and constantly enforced deference? Might we espouse the concept of reciprocal reinforcement: human and non-human taking turns as giver and receiver of reinforcement, both acting in ways that fulfill each other's desires?

This, though, runs the risk of messing up the sacrosanct hierarchy of "human dominates/outranks dog." Good. Out with this dogma! Give up your devotion to hierarchiology (a great term coined by Dr. Laurence J. Peter and Raymond Hull in their 1969 book, *The Peter Principle*). Consider rank (hierarchy) rank (stale and smelly).

But without our trusty paradigm of "humans are alpha," we may fear all will be chaos. Without hierarchy, aren't we left with anarchy? Fortunately, no. We can opt for heterarchy. Technically, this is a formal structure without any single permanent uppermost node. As applied to dog training, it means there is a flow of information and reinforcement (i.e., communication) back and forth between human and dog. It's circular rather than linear (i.e., from human to dog only). It encourages moving, behaving, and living rather than withdrawing, avoiding and submitting.

Of course, hierarchies have their place. I worked for the U.S. Navy. I understand the value of a chain of command in life-threatening situations. My model for training animals is not militaristic, though; it's not boot camp (though this term is so commonly used in dog-training articles and business names that it qualifies as a cliché).

Instead, my model is an expanded version of TEFL: Teaching English as a Foreign Language. In this case, it's more like "Teaching Human as a Foreign Lifestyle." Dogs are surrounded by humans who behave in distinctly non-canine ways. We use language constantly, emitting streams of sounds mostly unintelligible to dogs. Dogs not only don't understand English (or Italian, Norwegian, etc.); their verbal-language comprehension skills are rudimentary at best (despite the incredible toy-name comprehension abilities of amazing Border Collies Rico, Betsy and Chaser. See Recommended Reading).

One more source of puzzlement: we require our dogs to behave in all manner of unnatural ways. We want them to walk by our sides at a glacially slow pace, attached to us by a four-foot length of leather; to ignore dead squirrels—or live ones, for that matter; to greet people by sitting still; to come to us when called away from playing with doggie pals; and myriad other behaviors that dogs surely deem absurd.

So, above all but nutrition and shelter, dogs need translators—cultural liaisons and advocates to help them make sense of the mystery of living with humans. They have no innate knowledge of what we want and limited natural skill at comprehending our attempts to tell them. It's as if dogs have to piece together a complex jigsaw puzzle without ever having seen the image on the box cover. Dogs don't see the big picture—our final behavioral goals for "good manners." But dogs are behaviorally malleable—remarkably so, especially when young. Using patient, systematic training, we can help them put the pieces in place.

I recently experienced first-hand the vital role a translator can play. I was teaching a seminar in Italy (lucky me) where most of the students were not fluent in English. I don't speak Italian. I was assigned a translator, Francesca, who transformed my spoken English into Italian, and who restated the students' many questions in English for me. She also accompanied me during meals and on a day-trip to Verona.

Francesca was marvelous: skilled, kind, funny and tireless. I quickly realized that I not only valued her talent at turning my stream-of-consciousness lecture style into coherent Italian, but I relaxed whenever she was at my side. I could rely on her to help me interpret everything I needed to know about this foreign culture and its unique customs and behavioral expectations. My anxiety about making a gaffe or about being unable to communicate with students or shopkeepers evaporated when I was with my patient, caring translator. I felt deep empathy for our dogs, who must learn to comprehend and negotiate the behavioral intricacies of not just another nationality, but another species.

Can dogs ever act in the role of translator for us? Certainly, especially in tasks for which they are the experts. Dear old Effie and I recently completed an introductory NoseWork class. She excelled at sniffing out the hidden treats. Conversely, I had to work hard at staying out of her way and letting her natural skills blossom. My role wasn't to help her perform the search; it was mostly to drive her to class each week.

This is one small example of a context where by stepping back from the lead role—by letting my olfactorily-superior partner "take control"—I end up being a better trainer. Dogs excel in other skills, too, if we let them: playing, living in the present, speaking without words, paying attention to the discreet body language of companions and not paying attention to people's physical beauty, bank account or job title. By ditching the edict of "humans lead, dogs follow," I allow my own life to be enriched by an ongoing behavioral dialogue with another mind, another perspective.

Successful relationships are grounded in the essential dignity that flows as a by-product of this shared power, with each partner sometimes ceding the upper hand. Besides, the world surely doesn't need another dictator, benign or otherwise. But it never has enough lovers.

A couple of pointers

One last story. In my neighborhood, I've seen a young woman walking with her two German Shorthaired Pointers. One dog is always on her right, the other on her left. I've never seen either dog even a half-pace forging or lagging. This is even more noteworthy because they are off-leash while the woman pays no noticeable attention to them, instead often talking or texting on her phone. The dogs remain in perfect position as the woman changes direction, but they never seem to show any emotion. Their heads hang a bit low, their stubby tails point stiffly backward and their gait has no bounce. In fact, the dogs look almost unreal, like large liver-colored panniers attached to her hips.

I've watched this trio with interest, at first wondering if there was any way she could have trained such joyless perfection without using punishment (from some version of correction collar). I concluded that a person could use clicker-training (i.e., differential reinforcement that uses a behavioral marker) to teach the precise positioning, but not the blunted affect. Later, with genuine sadness, I realized that for many people watching this woman amid her flawless dogs, this would seem the epitome of animal training. Imagine, the dogs are behaving so robotically that the woman need not even look at them. Lucky her, they might think; she's free to catch up on her correspondence.

I also walk my dogs—Effie on my left and Nick on my right—nearly every day in my neighborhood. But their behavior bears little resemblance to the Pointers. Effie and Nick routinely walk a pace ahead of me, usually, but not always, keeping leashes slack. They often smell or see interesting stuff along the way, and sometimes one or the other will ask me, through their behavior, if we can stop to check it out. Sometimes I comply. I, too, see and hear interesting things along the way (e.g., recently, a bald eagle sitting in a low tree branch eating the duck it had just plucked out of Commencement Bay), and so I often ask my dogs to stop with me while I watch.

The thrill of the walk for all three of us is the mutual discovery of treasure, the shared experience of fresh air and novel stimuli. Occasionally, someone passing our trio will say to me, "Who's walking who?" (a phrase I despise for its narrow view of leadership, its general nastiness and its ungrammaticality). Our walks together are often the highlight of my day. My dogs' on-leash behavior isn't perfect, but I honestly don't find this problematic. Considering that both dogs have a long-ago history of being aggressive (Effie to dogs on leash, Nick to men anywhere), this is saying something. I gladly relinquish the chance to have Stepford dogs—mindlessly obedient and lacking humor—in exchange for the vibrant, silly, somewhat unpredictable dogs by my side.

The best trick of all

Many years ago, I had a little sign on my desk that said, "The more people I meet, the more I like my dog." It seemed humorous. I now recognize it as a manifestation of my own carefully hidden hostility and low self-esteem. After all, it's not exactly enlightened to disparage your own species. This same sentiment crops up too often among dog trainers who strive mightily for the welfare of their beloved canine students while covertly (or overtly) showing contempt for their "stupid" human clients.

It's a laudable goal to save the lives of dogs at risk of euthanasia due to behavioral problems. It's not enough, however, when dog trainers and animal behaviorists and veterinary staff are in an ideal position to accomplish so much more through their work with pet owners. They can change the way people engage with each other and their world. They can model non-violence in all interactions. They can promote behavior-modification techniques that honor dogs and honor the dogs' human caretakers as well.

Imagine if our primary goal for each dog-training lesson, class or consultation was to increase the comfort and joy of every creature in the room: dogs, human students and trainers. In addition to saving the lives of troubled dogs, we would strive to save the lives and promote the well-being of the stressed, struggling people in our care. The very purpose of our training would be less about using coercion to take choices away from our dogs and more about using positive reinforcement to clearly communicate which choices work; less about rationing our affection and interactions and more about reciprocal reinforcement and mutual play; less about "don't you dare do that" and more about "I dare you to try that!" This might free us to loosen our stranglehold on controlling our dogs' every pleasure, thereby discovering that despite our deep fear that all would be chaos without us In Charge, all will actually be okay. Radically so. What a relief—for us and everyone around us.

I'm not entirely naïve. I know well that behavior problems are often complex and that changing a dog's behavior can be hard. This doesn't mean that the changer has to be hard, too. We can allow our dogs to perform their best trick of all—cracking open our too-defended human hearts—without sacrificing any of our training goals. Profound behavioral transformations can then spring forth in both species: dogs becoming more civilized, people becoming more compassionate.

There is a simple parable, often attributed to the Cherokee. It tells of a young Cherokee man brought before the tribal elders who are concerned about his aggressive tendencies. One of the elders takes the young man aside and tells him that his anger is understandable, since all humans have within them two wolves. One wolf is generous, humble and open-hearted. The other is aggressive, arrogant and selfish. The two wolves are in constant battle with one another, since neither is powerful enough to destroy the other. The young man asks, "But which wolf will win?" The elder replies, "The one you feed."

It's your choice, through your routine daily actions, which wolf you feed. Dog training is an integral part of the lives of millions of people; it serves as a conduit for the daily feeding of one of the wolves. Which training philosophies and methods you embrace will determine which wolf grows. Choose well.

ABOUT THE AUTHOR

Kathy Sdao is an Associate Certified Applied Animal Behaviorist who has spent 26 years as a full-time animal trainer. As part of her work toward earning a master's degree in experimental psychology, Kathy trained dolphins at the University of Hawaii's Kewalo Basin Marine Mammal Laboratory. She went on to train dolphins for the United States Department of Defense and to train whales and walruses at the Point Defiance Zoo & Aquarium in Tacoma Washington. Since 1998, Kathy has owned and managed Bright Spot Dog Training, which provides behavior-modification services for pet owners. She teaches about a dozen seminars annually, for trainers around the world. DVDs of many of these seminars are available for purchase at www.kathysdao.com

Recommended Reading

Books

Clicker Basics for Dogs & Puppies, Carolyn Barney, 2007.

Clickertraining: The Four Secrets of Becoming a Supertrainer, Morten Egtvedt & Cecilie Køeste, 2008. Download available at http://www.canisclickertraining.com/clickertraining/

Clinical Behavioral Medicine for Small Animals, Karen Overall, 1997.

Coercion and its Fallout, Murray Sidman, 2000. (Available at www.behavior.org/item.php?id=150)

The Culture Clash, Jean Donaldson, 2005.

Curly Girl: The Handbook, Lorraine Massey, 2011.

Dogs: A New Understanding of Canine Origin, Behavior, and Evolution, Raymond & Lorna Coppinger, 2002.

Don't Shoot the Dog!: The New Art of Teaching and Training, Karen Pryor, 2006.

Falling Upward: A Spirituality for the Two Halves of Life, Richard Rohr, 2011. (Or most any other book by Fr. Rohr)

Handbook of Applied Dog Behavior and Training, Vol. 3: Procedures and Protocols, Steven R. Lindsay, 2005.

In Defense of Food: An Eater's Manifesto, Michael Pollan, 2009.

Made to Stick: Why Some Ideas Survive and Others Die, Chip Heath and Dan Heath, 2007.

Manpo-Kei: The Art and Science of Step Counting, Catrine Tudor-Locke, 2006.

The Psychology of B F Skinner, William T. O'Donohue & Kyle E. Ferguson, 2001.

The Relationship Cure: A 5 Step Guide to Strengthening Your Marriage, Family, and Friendships, John Gottman, 2002. (www.gottman.com)

Ruff Love: A Relationship Building Program for You and Your Dog, Susan Garrett, 2002.

The Thinking Dog: Crossover to Clicker Training, Gail Tamases Fisher, 2009.

Why We Get Fat: And What to Do About It, Gary Taubes, 2010.

Articles
Friedman, S. G. (2008) "What's wrong with this picture? Effectiveness is not enough." *Good Bird Magazine,* Vol 4-4. (Dr. Friedman's excellent website is www.behaviorworks.org; her online course in behavior analysis—"Living & Learning with Animals"—is a not-to-be-missed learning opportunity for all animal trainers and veterinary professionals.)

Kaminski, J., Call J. & Fischer, J. (2004) "Word learning in a domestic dog: Evidence for 'fast mapping.'" *Science,* 304, 1682–1683.

Mech, L. D. (1999) "Alpha status, dominance, and division of labor in wolf packs." *Canadian Journal of Zoology,* 77:(8) 1196–203.

Morell, V. (March 2008) "Minds of their own." *National Geographic,* 36–61.

Pilley, J.W. & Reid, A. K. (2011) "Border collie comprehends object names as verbal referents." *Behavioural Processes,* 86, 184–195.

Schwarz, J. (2001) "Emotional bids are key, Gottman finds." *University Week* (publication of the University of Washington), May 10, 2001. (http://depts.washington.edu/uweek/archives/2001.05.MAY_10/_article11.html)

Udell, M.A.R. & Wynne, C.D.L. (2008) "A review of domestic dogs' (Canis familiaris) human-like behaviors: Or why behavior analysts should stop worrying and love their dogs." *Journal of the Experimental Analysis of Behavior,* 89(2): 247–261.

www.dogwise.com   1-800-776-2665

Selected titles from Dogwise Publishing

BEHAVIOR & TRAINING

Aggression In Dogs. Practical Mgmt, Prevention, & Behaviour Modification. Brenda Aloff

Am I Safe? DVD. Sarah Kalnajs

Barking. The Sound of a Language. Turid Rugaas

Between Dog and Wolf. Understanding the Connection and the Confusion. Jessica Addams and Andrew Miller

Canine Behavior. A Photo Illustrated Handbook. Barbara Handelman

Canine Body Language. A Photographic Guide to the Native Language of Dogs. Brenda Aloff

Chill Out Fido! How to Calm Your Dog. Nan Arthur

Clicked Retriever. Lana Mitchell

Do Over Dogs. Give Your Dog a Second Chance for a First Class Life. Pat Miller

Dogs are from Neptune. Jean Donaldson

Evolution of Canine Social Behavior, 2nd ed. Roger Abrantes

Language of Dogs, DVD. Sarah Kalnajs

My Dog Pulls. What Do I Do? Turid Rugaas

Oh Behave! Dogs from Pavlov to Premack to Pinker. Jean Donaldson

On Talking Terms with Dogs. Calming Signals, 2nd edition. Turid Rugaas

On Talking Terms with Dogs. What Your Dog Tells You, DVD. Turid Rugaas

Play With Your Dog. Pat Miller

Positive Perspectives. Love Your Dog, Train Your Dog. Pat Miller

Positive Perspectives 2. Know Your Dog, Train Your Dog. Pat Miller

Stress in Dogs. Martina Scholz & Clarissa von Reinhardt

Tales of Two Species. Essays on Loving and Living With Dogs. Patricia McConnell

The Dog Trainer's Resource. The APDT Chronicle of the Dog Collection. Mychelle Blake (*ed*)

The Dog Trainer's Resource 2. The APDT Chronicle of the Dog Collection. Mychelle Blake (*ed*)

The Thinking Dog. Crossover to Clicker Training. Gail Fisher

Therapy Dogs. Training Your Dog To Reach Others. Kathy Diamond Davis

When Pigs Fly. Train Your Impossible Dog. Jane Killion

HEALTH & ANATOMY, SHOWING

An Eye for a Dog. Illustrated Guide to Judging Purebred Dogs. Robert Cole

Another Piece of the Puzzle. Pat Hastings

Canine Massage. A Complete Reference Manual. Jean-Pierre Hourdebaigt

The Canine Thyroid Epidemic. W. Jean Dodds and Diana Laverdure

Dog Show Judging. The Good, the Bad, and the Ugly. Chris Walkowicz

The Healthy Way to Stretch Your Dog. A Physical Theraphy Approach. Sasha Foster and Ashley Foster

It's a Dog Not a Toaster. Finding Your Fun in Competitive Obedience. Diana Kerew

Puppy Intensive Care. A Breeder's Guide To Care Of Newborn Puppies. Myra Savant Harris

Raw Dog Food. Make It Easy for You and Your Dog. Carina MacDonald

Raw Meaty Bones. Tom Lonsdale

Shock to the System. The Facts About Animal Vaccination... Catherine O'Driscoll

Tricks of the Trade. From Best of Intentions to Best in Show, Rev. Ed. Pat Hastings

Work Wonders. Feed Your Dog Raw Meaty Bones. Tom Lonsdale

Whelping Healthy Puppies, DVD. Sylvia Smart

Dogwise.com is your complete source for dog books on the web!

2,000+ titles, fast shipping, and excellent customer service.

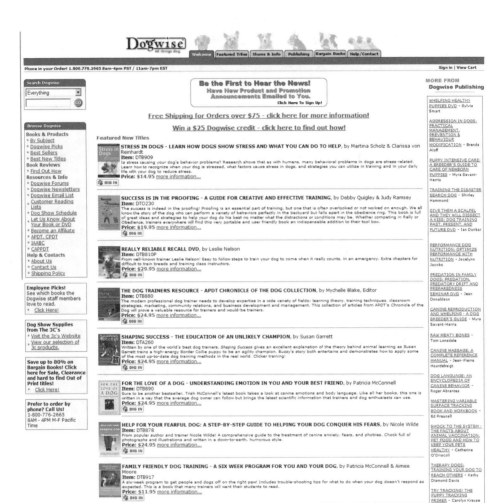